Collected Poems

Robert Hayden

Collected Poems

Edited by Frederick Glaysher

Liveright Publishing Corporation   New York / London

For information about permission to reproduce selections from this book, write
to Permissions, Liveright Publishing Corporation, 500 Fifth Avenue,
New York, NY 10110.

Composition and manufacturing by the Haddon Craftsmen, Inc.

ISBN 0-87140-651-9

Liveright Publishing Corporation, 500 Fifth Avenue, New York, N.Y. 10110.
W. W. Norton & Company Ltd., 10 Coptic Street, London WC1A 1PU

3 4 5 6 7 8 9 0

For Michael Tedla

Editor's Note

The typescript of *Words in the Mourning Time*, the master set and corrected page proofs of *Angle of Ascent*, and the manuscript of the 1982 edition of *American Journal* have been relied on, whenever possible, for all editorial decisions. According to Robert Hayden's expressed wishes, several poems have been restored, and one poem, "Bone-Flower Elegy," which he had held back from *American Journal* for another book, is published here for the first time. This text reflects, through restraint, Hayden's evaluation regarding his "'prentice pieces." The Notes are his.

Contents

Words in the Mourning Time (1970)

Introduction

It seems fair to say that with every passing year since his death in 1980 at the age of sixty-seven, our memory of the poet Robert Hayden threatens to slip deeper and deeper into obscurity. So it would be with all writers, unless each of us who love and value their work summons new readers to their texts. In Hayden's case, neglect would be truly unfortunate not simply because his verse is among the most accomplished to have been written in America in this century but also because, emerging out of a complex set of potentially destructive forces, his body of verse has much to offer us as we ourselves engage and are engaged by many of those forces. As an individual, Hayden was a man subjected virtually from the start of his life to harsh personal pressures that might easily have silenced someone less courageous. His work is further testimony to the power of the artist to find and illuminate the profoundly human in the midst of chaos, and to produce art as a bulwark against the will to inhumanity that is such an essential part of the human condition.

Robert Earl Hayden was born in Detroit, Michigan, on August 4, 1913, the son of Asa and Ruth Sheffey. His parents named him Asa Bundy Sheffey. Before he was two, however, their marriage collapsed and his mother, traveling in search of work, gave him up to a poor but respectable couple in the neighborhood, William and Sue Ellen Hayden. Although the child remained aware of the identity of his natural parents, saw them from time to time, and eventually became close once again with his mother, he grew up as a foster child of the Haydens, who renamed him and reared him as their son. He would discover only when he was forty, by accident, that they had never adopted him legally or even officially changed his name, although they had led him to believe that they had done both. His adoptive father, a laborer who sometimes had trouble finding work, was a disciplinarian and a dedicated Baptist. His adoptive mother, according to the Hayden scholar Pontheolla Taylor Williams, "regaled Robert with Afro-American folktales, stories of southern racial atrocities, and her own post-Civil War experiences, when she was a chambermaid on Ohio River steamers."

Robert Hayden was from the start a marked child. The Haydens treated him well, according to their lights, but their marriage was chronically strained by bickering and other forms of conflict about which the poet eventually wrote, most movingly perhaps in his compelling piece "Those Winter Sundays." Poor eyesight painfully and endlessly complicated his youth and, indeed, his entire life. He could not take part in sports, and his thick lenses made him an easy target for the cruelty of other children. Poverty prevented his parents from making more than a token attempt to develop his artistic interests, such as music, outside of school.

His experience of racial difference was bittersweet. Hayden passed his earliest years in a section of Detroit (later nicknamed Paradise Valley) that remained racially diverse until an influx of Southern blacks in search of jobs, followed by reactive white flight, turned it virtually all-black. His early familiarity with Jews, Germans, Italians, and other whites, reflected in several of his poems, perhaps laid the foundation for the transracial philosophy that is a hallmark of Hayden's art. Attending a mainly white high school, he felt both a degree of ostracism and, at the same time, a degree of acceptance and understanding support.

Hayden's myopia and the cruelty it often inspired drove him inward and toward books, where he soon discovered the particular solace of poetry. Midway through his teenage years he already knew the most popular of the modern writers, including whites such as Edna St. Vincent Millay and Carl Sandburg and blacks such as Langston Hughes and Countee Cullen. He was especially taken with the example of Countee Cullen, whose emotional and lyrical blending of race consciousness with traditional poetics left an immediate mark on Hayden's youthful writing.

Although he was also drawn to the theater, Hayden's commitment to writing verse was probably set by the time he left high school in 1930. His dedication only intensified when he attended, from 1932 to 1936, Detroit City College (later Wayne State University), where he met other writers who encouraged his ambitions. Langston Hughes, visiting the area for the production of one of his plays, further inspired Hayden. As with so many other American writers during the Depression, which he and his family felt to the point of pauperism, Hayden became attracted to radical socialism as a political philosophy. After college, he worked on the Federal Writers' Project, which encouraged his socialist leanings and, more importantly for his future as a poet, deepened his knowledge of African-American history, especially through his official research into antislavery activity in Michigan and into slave culture in general.

Strains of a socialist esthetic, as well as of a far more traditional approach to art, coexist uneasily in Hayden's first volume of verse, *Heart-Shape in the Dust*, which he published in 1940. The prevailing impression left by this volume is Hayden's imitativeness at this point in his career. Eventually he would regard almost all of these poems as immature and deny them a place in definitive collections of his work.

Also in 1940, Hayden married Erma Inez Morris, a gifted pianist and music teacher. Two years later, their only child, a daughter they named Maia, was born. Their marriage lasted until Hayden's death in 1980.

Probably neither Hughes nor Cullen was ultimately as large an influence on Hayden's mature art as was W. H. Auden. Hayden met Auden between 1941 and 1942, when Auden taught at the University of Michigan (Hayden was a student there from 1941 to 1946). Already an internationally famous poet, Auden steered Hayden in certain new directions. Auden had already repudiated his own earlier commitment to radical socialism, and Hayden now began to do the same. Increasingly he distanced himself from African-American cultural nationalism, with which he had been struggling as a force for some time, as Countee Cullen had struggled before him. Seeing Marxism and ultranationalism as, in different ways, inimical to the flourishing of art, Auden proposed a modernist poetry of technical and meditative complexity, in which judicious erudition and imagination, rather than pseudo-folk simplicity or didacticism, were vital elements. He encouraged in Hayden an appreciation of the work of British poets such as Hopkins, Hardy, and Yeats, as well as that of genuine contemporaries such as Spender. W. B. Yeats's highly sophisticated response to Irish history and culture, with all its controversies and passions, showed Hayden that a poet could become saturated in nationalistic lore and love and still maintain independence of vision. He once declared that he sought to be a black poet "the way Yeats is an Irish poet."

As Hayden engaged these new influences, he absorbed yet another decisive force of change. He turned aside finally from the Baptist faith of his adoptive father, in which he had been stringently brought up, and committed himself for the rest of his life to his wife's religion; he became a member of the Baha'i faith. In the Baha'i faith, with its belief in the unity of all religions, as well as in universal education, the equality of the sexes, simplicity of living, the possibilities of an international government and language, and a life of service to one's suffering fellow human beings, Hayden found an intellectual and spiritual source to which he could turn as he wrestled with the powers of despair and doubt, negativism and nihilism, to which he was habitually vulnerable. The Baha'i faith fostered in him a spiritually evolved and yet socially engaged sense of humanity and the poetic function. While some of his critics found the Baha'i faith a peculiar choice for a writer insisting on freedom from system and dogma, Hayden alluded lovingly to his religion in several poems, including "From the Corpse Woodpiles, from the Ashes." In "Words in the Mourning Time," he hails its prophet Bahá'v'lláh as "Logos, poet, cosmic hero, surgeon, architect / of our hope for peace."

Hayden's emergence as a mature human being and poet did not lead to public recognition. In fact, for the next twenty years or more he struggled to assert himself professionally. In 1946 he moved to Fisk University in Nashville, Tennessee, where he would teach English literature and, less frequently, creative writing until 1969. A heavy workload impeded his growth as a writer, although fellowships occasionally gave him respites and in 1954 allowed him to travel in Mexico (he had studied Spanish in college). Although he published little, his poems attracted a growing coterie of admirers.

Hayden also influenced a number of gifted young African-American writers at Fisk, including Myron O'Higgins and William Demby. With them he championed the need for an art free of crude propaganda and yet engaged with the realities of black American life; he also insisted on the importance of experimentation and innovation in art. Toward the end of his stay at Fisk, these views brought him into painful conflict with adherents of the new Black Power movement. Many of them openly rejected both Hayden's ideas and his art as outmoded, at best, and a form of racial treachery, at worst. In their view, the black poet must actively aid the revolution that was at hand. Refusing to compromise on his principles, rejecting "the chauvinistic and the doctrinaire," but unquestionably hurt by the controversy, Hayden went his own way.

About the same time, however, his career in other respects took a turn for the better. In 1966 he won the Grand Prize in Poetry at the First World Festival of Negro Arts in Dakar, Senegal. Also in 1966, Hayden published his *Selected Poems,* which brought him increased visibility as a writer. He began a series of visiting appointments at universities that culminated in his appointment in 1969 as a professor at the University of Michigan. Home at last, in a sense, Hayden taught there until his death in 1980. Between 1976 and 1978 he served two terms as poetry consultant to the Library of Congress, a position then regarded as tantamount to being appointed poet laureate of the United States.

In 1979, he was diagnosed as suffering from cancer, for which he declined to undergo chemotherapy. The following year, Hayden died.

• • •

About ninety poems make up this volume, *The Collected Poems of Robert Hayden.* Hayden published many more than that number during the course of his life. However, in editing this collection, Frederick Glaysher clearly followed the wishes of the poet in taking a strict, even severe approach to his " 'prentice pieces," as Hayden, in long retrospect, called the verse of *Heart-Shape in the Dust,* which is not represented here. *Collected Poems* also ignores Hayden's share of *The Lion and the Archer: Poems* (1948), published in collaboration with Myron O'Higgins, as well as Hayden's *Figure of Time* (1955). Well represented, however, are *A Ballad of Remembrance* (1962), a pamphlet of verse published by Paul Breman in London to inaugurate Breman's important Heritage series; *Selected Poems* (1966); *Words in the Mourning Time* (1970), which was nominated for a National Book Award, as widespread notice finally began to be taken of Hayden; *The Night-Blooming Cereus* (1972); *Angle of Ascent: New and Selected Poems* (1975), from Liveright, which marked Hayden's first appearance, after more than thirty-five years of writing poetry, with a major book publisher; and *American Journal* (1978), put out by Effendi Press largely on the initiative of Hayden's admirer, the poet Michael S. Harper. The poems of Hayden's last years were collected in a posthumously published (1982) volume, also called *American Journal,* from Liveright.

Hayden's *Collected Poems* offers the reader a relatively slender volume, especially given the fact that it represents the product of a career of some forty years. However, this is precisely as the poet wanted it to be. Hayden was a relentless polisher and honer, what used to be called (often with a mixture of admiration and rebuke) a "laborious" poet. In other words, he believed in the working and reworking of texts, rather than in the original, irresistible power of inspiration and improvisation in writing verse. If his work sometimes suggests a clear will towards monumentality, it also reveals at the same time an appreciation for limits. Most of

Hayden's poems do not exhaust a page, and even his several multipart pieces are relatively brief in totality. The amount of poetry he left behind reflects in some degree the personal and professional difficulties he faced as he strove to make a living for himself and his family. However, the polished conciseness of his *Collected Poems* also speaks to the high standards of craftsmanship by which he deliberately lived as a poet. Thus distilled, the quality of his verse in this volume should be more than sufficient to ensure the continuing of his reputation as one of the main pillars of African-American poetry and also one of the more compelling talents among all American writers of his time, regardless of race.

To consider Hayden first as an African-American poet, then as an American poet, may appear to reopen needlessly one of the more troubling questions concerning him, as well as to risk violating his abiding wish that he should be seen not as a black poet but simply as a poet. Yet Hayden has little to fear from the reopening, which may be essential, given the realities of American culture. Like Cullen, Hayden was highly sensitive on the question of the relationship between race and poetry; both were appalled by any attempt to foreclose the range of a poet who happened to be born black. However, while Cullen found an achingly poignant contradiction between blackness in America and the poetic vocation (God had done, he writes in one place, "a curious thing, / To make a poet black and bid him sing!"), Hayden early came to a resolution of this tension.

Probably no other black poet of his age surpassed Hayden in the unconditional nature of his love of the English language. For many writers sensitive to the relationship between language and political power, the English language, and the canonical status of much English literature, can be a constant disturbance. Paul Laurence Dunbar, for instance, never reconciled his work in black dialect, which he both loved and despised, with his productions in standard English. ("A jingle in a broken tongue," he called the former in one poem.) Langston Hughes sought deeper meanings in "black" forms of speech and music, although he also wrote in standard English. In the case of Gwendolyn Brooks, the high-modernist eloquence (yoked uncomfortably, she came to believe, to her often racial subject matter) that won her the Pulitzer Prize and other honors gave way to the didactic, street-inflected verse that followed her acceptance of the Black Power movement in the 1960s.

While its specific Biblical allusions are few, Hayden's poetry proclaims virtually everywhere his faith in the orthodox or "classical" language of the authors of the King James Bible and of the major English poets of the early seventeenth century. Sometimes his syntax is contorted, and arcane words stud his texts from time to time; sometimes a blues or jazz riff enlivens the rhythms of his poetic discourse. On the whole, however, he was at peace writing in standard English. Over the course of his career he favored various styles. At times, his diction is complex and highly ornate; in another mode it is restrained and even austere; in yet another, he shows a sure ability to render verse in an easy colloquial manner that is remarkable, given the intricately formal diction he employs elsewhere.

He also revealed early an absolute sense of comfort with the tradition of British and American literature, black and white. "When I was in college," Hayden recalled, "I read all the poetry I could get hold of, and I read without discrimination." He took full advantage of a situation probably not available to a black American, in any real sense, before his time. He was aware not only of writers of the Harlem Renaissance but also of the beloved, older work of Paul Laurence

Dunbar ("Poet of our youth— / his 'cri du coeur' our own"). Hayden would make the most of this patrimony even as he moved to absorb the work of poets in the wider world.

It is possible to see Hayden both as a preeminently racial poet and as one ultimately transcending race. The Dutch scholar Rosey Pool, who worked hard to bring his work to the attention of European readers, liked to call him the "poet laureate" of the race (a title that Langston Hughes, for one, coveted). On the other hand, the late Michael Cooke, in his study *The Achievement of Intimacy in Afro-American Literature,* gave Hayden pride of place among all black poets in this century mainly because of his ability to absorb, then transcend, racial feeling. Among modern black poets, Cooke argued, Hayden epitomized a supreme "sense of purpose arising *from within* and expressing an organic, vibrant humanity rather than a formal, plastic institutionality. The result has been a simultaneous manifestation of passivity and militancy, fused in another dimension."

Hayden came to accept the African-American past as an inexhaustible, primary poetic resource, rather than as a badge of shame, as it sometimes appears in Cullen's writing. Almost half of the poems in his first volume, *Heart-Shape in the Dust,* acknowledge race in one form or another, and Hayden would persist in writing memorable poems on the subject of African-American history and culture even as he became more complex as a thinker and more accomplished as an artist. Indeed, Hayden is best known for his historical poems, and above all those on African-American history. Pieces such as his sonnet "Frederick Douglass," his meditation on slavery "Middle Passage," his blues-haunted paean to Bessie Smith "Homage to the Empress of the Blues," as well as other pieces on slavery, racism, history, and African-American culture, repeatedly anthologized, confirm Hayden's profound commitment to the culture out of which he had come, even as he was also committed to linking the particularities of black culture to the universal concerns of the human condition. Rather than emphasize the power of racial feeling, he dwelt instead on the actualities of history and culture, even as those actualities became the launching place for his flights of imagination and intelligence.

In engaging African-American history and culture as a poet, Hayden was aware of the pitfalls often presented to the modern artist by folk art and folk culture. Rather than patronize the folk, he inevitably interpreted poetic modernism to mean mainly the subordination of folk or street culture to "high" culture, and by distinctly privileging the language of the latter over that of the former. This was no inconsequential move for an African-American writer, especially one who also favored the more egalitarian approach of poets such as Hughes and Sterling Brown. Certain poems based in the black experience, such as "Witch Doctor" (which mocks a black preacher-charlatan), "Aunt Jemima of the Ocean Waves," and even the majestic "Homage to the Empress of the Blues," look down on mass culture from a certain height. Hayden was determined to subject all experience to the scrutiny of the intellect and the imagination fully empowered. However, he also developed, as Robert M. Greenberg has pointed out, a remarkable technique that involves the subtle, sometimes almost imperceptible fusion of a folk character, on the one hand, and the narrator's voice, on the other. This fusion allowed him to explore and develop his investment in folklore to the best of his ability, but without overpowering the folk material.

In his often anthologized piece "A Ballad of Remembrance," set in New Orleans at Mardi Gras, the speaker of the poem reels in dazed disgust before the surrealistic grotesqueries of Mardi Gras. In an example of the ornate stylistic mode that he himself called "baroque," Hayden stunningly captures, with a dazzling array of images of chaos and corruption, the peculiar horror of New Orleans in history ("the down-South arcane city with death / in its jaws like gold teeth"). Then, with his language suddenly subsiding into calm and lucidity, the speaker is rescued from all this disaster by the arrival of a friend, the critic Mark Van Doren, who is named. "Then you arrived," the poem recalls, "meditative, ironic, / richly human; and your presence was shore where I rested / released from the hoodoo of that dance, where I spoke / with my true voice again." Few American poets, perhaps, would have the courage or even the desire to make so ringing a declaration of humanistic values in a similar situation. Hayden judges contemporary culture as he would judge history, without compromise or fear of censure on political grounds.

History is of supreme importance to him as a poet. The five poems that conclude the first section of *Collected Poems,* which is from *A Ballad of Remembrance,* are all inspired by African-American history: "Middle Passage," about the vessels that brought unhappy blacks to America ("Shuttles in the rocking loom of history, / the dark ships move"); "O Daedalus, Fly Away Home," an entrancing merger of classical and African-American slave myths about ambition, freedom, and flight; "The Ballad of Nat Turner," a chilling poetic monologue by the violent slave insurrectionist of 1831 in Virginia ("Lord God my harshener, / speak to me now or let me die"); "Runagate Runagate," about a desperate search by a runaway slave for free ground ("Runs falls rises stumbles on from darkness into darkness"); and the sonnet "Frederick Douglass," with its cleverly orchestrated anticipation of the arrival at last (as the sonnet ends) of "this freedom, this liberty, this beautiful / and terrible thing, needful to man as air, / usable as earth."

By the 1960s, when assassinations and insurrections in America made ordinary time, even the passage of a few weeks or months, appear to resound with the lessons of history, Hayden had mastered the historic view, which is to say his prophetic ability to interpret the present in terms of both the past and the future. A small masterpiece in this regard is "El-Hajj Malik El-Shabazz," an elegy in four parts on the death in 1965 of the most militant black leader of the civil rights era, the former Nation of Islam minister Malcolm X, who, following a pilgrimage to Mecca, turned away from the racial hatreds explicit in his former religion to embrace Islamic orthodoxy. Hayden celebrates this illumination even as he mourns the violence—historical and personal—that preceded and followed it. Malcolm, who had "X'd his name, became his people's anger, / exhorted them to vengeance for their past," had lived long enough to possess a more formidable truth: "He fell upon his face before / Allah the raceless in whose blazing Oneness all / were one. He rose renewed renamed, became / much more than there was time for him to be."

With such poems, one is tempted to see Hayden working as a kind of historical muralist. The reason or reasons for Hayden's affinity for the form may run deeper than a delight in history, or a sense of the peculiar significance of history to African Americans. It may be that Hayden tightly embraced black history, where the moral questions are conveniently stark, with something of a sense of release from having to reveal more about himself as an individual. Although he lived through the heyday of what is called "confessional" poetry, he appears to have had a genuine anxiety about poetry based on intimate personal revelation. "I could never write," he once said, "the confessional poems that Anne Sexton, Robert Lowell, [and] John Berryman have become identified with." He added: "Reticence has its aesthetic value too."

Reticence can also be dangerous for a poet. Reticence in addition to Hayden's conservative sense of language and of literary tradition, as well as the potential mildness of the Baha'i religion, could easily have added up to a career of torpid verse. This is clearly not the case here. But what, if anything, did Hayden believe he had to hide with his reticence? Pontheolla Taylor Williams, who regularly corresponded with him in the course of her research into his life and art, has identified homoeroticism and bisexuality—which Hayden never publicly acknowledged—as a troubling source of guilt and shame for the poet. She cites poems such as "Sphinx," " 'Mystery Boy' Looks for Kin in Nashville," and "The Mirages" as works in which Hayden engages, but only behind a thick concealing veil, his lifelong fears pertaining to his sexuality. This may well be so. For an individual of Hayden's professional standing in the African-American community, confessionalism that would reveal such interests was virtually not an option. When Hayden uses the details of his life as the core of a poem—and it is seldom absolutely clear that he is doing so—those details are heavily attended by invention and imagination so as to conceal the actual life of the poet himself.

Nevertheless, his nonhistorical poetry is anything but mild. From the start, Hayden struggled as a writer with a harrowing vision of human nature, a vision that finally eclipses in importance even racism as a power in his life and in life in general—although the relationship between racism and such a vision, in an African American, is perhaps necessarily symbiotic at some level. Most of Hayden's poems between the 1940s and the 1960s seem to have at their core some act of violence or of actual or potential volatility, whose destructive potential is fearsome. Such poems typically begin in a specific act or situation of brutality, from which the poet moves scrupulously toward a conclusion, marked but undogmatic, about human nature and the world. In "The Lions," a late poem, he writes of that "savage real that clues / my vision of the real— / my soul exults and Holy cries / and Holy Holy cries." The "savage real" is central to Hayden's vision and his poetry, which may be seen essentially as an act of containment, a "reflex of life-wish" (as he puts it in "The Diver"), that permits the "measured rise" from the cold, gloomy, fatally infested depths of experience.

Where this sense of violence came from is unclear. In a thinly veiled autobiographical reference to his youth, he recalls in one place "the chronic angers of that house," as he grew up in the Hayden household; ultimately, no doubt, he was referring to all the twisted conflicts and anxieties that plagued him early in life. This immersion in violence, albeit mainly psychological, was evidently enough to stamp in Hayden's mind a fascination with it and, transcendently, with its illuminations. In "Electrical Storm" ("seeing the lightning's / Mene Mene Tekel, / hearing the preaching thunder's deep / Upharsin"), the terror is natural and yet supernatural; the poet is numbed by the thought of the casual imperatives of death. In "The Rabbi," when "the synagogue became / New Calvary" and Hirschel and Molly, his friends, vanish before the scourge of urban change, the source of pain is human, societal, but no more explicable. In "Night, Death, Mississippi," the source is topical, regional. Here the poet allows an old white man, willing but too decrepit to assist anymore in a lynching, to welcome home those who have just done so. In "Incense of the Lucky Virgin," where a deranged black woman tries superstition and prayers to bring back her husband, then apparently slaughters her "daddyless" children ("Cleola, Willie Mae / won't be hungry any more, / oh they'll never cry and hunger any more"), the seed of the poem is only an item of journalism perhaps, yet it is no less vibrant in Hayden's depiction of despair and insane resolve.

In Hayden's world, violence is the central contagion. Violence subverts, infects, poisons. In "The Whipping," an old woman flogs a boy ("Wildly he crashes through elephant ears, / pleads in dusty zinnias"). The child's echoing, fruitless pleas haunt the poet ("His tears are rainy weather / to woundlike memories"). Exhausted at last, the woman leans against a tree, ". . . purged— / avenged in part for lifelong hidings / she has had to bear." In "Perseus," the mythological hero beheads Medusa, only to thirst for more blood: "None could have passed me then— / no garland-bearing girl, no priest / or staring boy—and lived." In "From the Corpse Woodpiles, from the Ashes," destruction is genocidal, global. The faces of Dachau ("O David, Hirschel, Eva, / cops and robbers with me once, / their faces are like yours") are also like the faces in Johannesburg, Seoul, and, no doubt, America: "Their struggles are all horizons. / Their deaths encircle me."

Violence is everywhere, but Hayden's sense of the uses of violence evolved over his life. Early in his career, and in the context of African-American history and the desire for freedom, violence is often seen as a necessary evil. The violence of African-American history, mostly endured by blacks, sometimes inflicted by blacks in retaliation, then kept the poet from an easy embrace of pacifism. In "Middle Passage," about the historic revolt of African slaves, led by the courageous Cinquez, on the ship *Amistad*, Hayden hails "The deep immortal human wish, / the timeless will: / Cinquez its deathless primaveral image, / life that transfigures many lives." Nor does the poet censure Nat Turner, who, transfigured from slave to murderous insurrectionist, "praised my honer, harshener / till a sleep came over me, / a sleep heavy as death." The poet leaves Turner biding his time, awaiting the inflicting of slaughter. The slave in "Runagate Runagate" has the last word: "Mean mean mean to be free."

In *A Ballad of Remembrance*, freedom is the essence of life, and blood spilled in its behalf is blood nobly spilled. Perhaps a poem on the prophet of the Baha'i faith, "Bahá'u'lláh in the Garden of Ridwan," puts rage into philosophic perspective: "Agonies confirm His hour, / and swords like compass-needles turn / toward His heart." This approach gives way, by the appearance in 1970 of Hayden's *Words in the Mourning Time*, to a sense of the absolute futility of violence. Hayden openly disdains any ameliorative claims, especially those by political revolutionists, on behalf of bloodshed. By this time, as exemplified in a poem such as "Zeus over Redeye," after Hayden's visit to a missile arsenal, he also saw technology itself as the Medusa-like twentieth-century sibling of violence.

By the time he came to write his elegy for Malcolm X, as we have seen, Hayden would absolutely oppose violence. In *Words in the Mourning Time*, although violence remains central to the text, the main energy of the poems seeks to serve not only the elegiac but also the curbing of our will to suicide. The national horror is not easily transcended, but mourning is a necessary step toward that transcendence: ". . . for King for Kennedy I mourn. / And for America, self-destructive, self-betrayed." Grief is, nevertheless, a

xxxi

"vanity." The Baha'i faith ("The Blessed Exile's / transil-luminating word") teaches that these agonies are "process, major means whereby, / oh dreadfully, our humanness must be achieved." In such a time, art can console and enlighten where little else can. In poems such as "The Peacock Room," which is one of Hayden's finest, he proclaims the power of art to give meaning to life. In "Monet's 'Waterli-lies,' " if "the news from Selma and Saigon / poisons the air like fallout," the poet takes refuge in the presence of "the serene great picture that I love": "Here space and time exist in light / the eye like the eye of faith believes."

> O light beheld as through refracting tears.
> Here is the aura of that world
>   each of us has lost.
> Here is the shadow of its joy.

Hayden's verse reflects a profound regret about the myr-iad ways in which the will to destroy makes beauty and clar-ity almost impossible in the world, which must survive through refractions and paradoxes rather than through a serene apprehension of reality. Yet the heroic determination to survive and to assert the human is also a hallmark of his art. The brilliant seven poems of *The Night-Blooming Cereus,* especially the title poem, confirm Hayden's ability to suffer and see more clearly for his suffering—even if what he sees above all is his and our ultimate inability to see clearly, as in "Traveling through Fog": ". . . the cloudy dark / ensphering us seems all we can / be certain of. Is Plato's cave." The flower of the title poem becomes the sadly re-duced spirit of the world, the speaker a humbled pleader on its behalf. "Lunar presence, / foredoomed, already dying," the night-blooming cereus flower "charged the room." The observers are rendered speechless: "We spoke / in whispers when / we spoke / at all. . . ."

Aptly titled, *Angle of Ascent* (1975) marks a kind of lift-off in the arc of Hayden's art. Curiously, it includes his autobiographical "Beginnings," in five parts, as if to signal that he can advance only by going backward to his origins. The tension between remembered terror and a dawning serenity is, at times, acute. Perhaps the evolved figure of the poet emerges most starkly in "For a Young Artist." Central to the poem is "a naked old man / with bloodstained wings," who flops about ignominiously but finally, magically, hears "silken rustling in the air, / the angle of ascent / achieved." Hayden's concern is more and more cosmic, even fantastic, and yet it is brought down to earth by the din of public events in the decade (wars and rumors of wars, assassinations and famine, and—above all—the threat of nuclear annihilation). The poet finds irony and paradox in the onward rush of civilization toward destruction. An intensified hunger for meaning and for fresh inspiration haunts the aging Hayden as it haunted the aging Yeats. In Hayden's "Stars," itself in five fragmentary parts, the poet questions: "How shall the mind keep warm / save at spectral / fires— how thrive but by the light / of paradox?"

To the end, Hayden remained an inspired poet, one who chose to define himself in the largest way possible but also fastened himself and his craft to the realities of his place and time and history. He saw himself, in his central identity, as an American poet. His persistent recognition of violence is perhaps the main token of this identity. Hayden knew his country and its condition, and saw it whole. He paid America the tribute of a scrupulous and interrogatory art, but did not hesitate also to show America his love. *American Journal,* his last major attempt at poetry, found him settled in the persona of a visitor from outer space, evaluating the natives:

confess i am curiously drawn   unmentionable   to
the americans   doubt i could exist among them for
long however   psychic demands far too severe
much violence   much that repels   i am attracted
none the less   their variousness their ingenuity
their elan vital   and that some thing   essence
quiddity   i cannot penetrate or name

Arnold Rampersad
Princeton University

A Ballad of Remembrance (1962), (1966)

For
Betsy Graves Reyneau
and
Beryl Parker

For Erma,
again and always,
and for Maia,
our daughter

The Diver

Sank through easeful
azure. Flower
creatures flashed and
shimmered there—
lost images
fadingly remembered.
Swiftly descended
into canyon of cold
nightgreen emptiness.
Freefalling, weightless
as in dreams of
wingless flight,
plunged through infra-
space and came to
the dead ship,
carcass that swarmed with
voracious life.
Angelfish, their
lively blue and
yellow prised from
darkness by the
flashlight's beam,
thronged her portholes.
Moss of bryozoans
blurred, obscured her
metal. Snappers,
gold groupers explored her,
fearless of bubbling
manfish. I entered
the wreck, awed by her silence,
feeling more keenly
the iron cold.
With flashlight probing
fogs of water

saw the sad slow
dance of gilded
chairs, the ectoplasmic
swirl of garments,
drowned instruments
of buoyancy,
drunken shoes. Then
livid gesturings,
eldritch hide and
seek of laughing
faces. I yearned to
find those hidden
ones, to fling aside
the mask and call to them,
yield to rapturous
whisperings, have
done with self and
every dinning
vain complexity.
Yet in languid
frenzy strove, as
one freezing fights off
sleep desiring sleep;
strove against the
cancelling arms that
suddenly surrounded
me, fled the numbing
kisses that I craved.
Reflex of life-wish?
Respirator's brittle
belling? Swam from
the ship somehow;
somehow began the
measured rise.

4

Electrical Storm
(for Arna and Alberta)

God's angry with the world again,
the grey neglected ones would say;
He don't like ugly.
Have mercy, Lord, they prayed,
seeing the lightning's
Mene Mene Tekel,
hearing the preaching thunder's deep
Upharsin.
They hunched up, contracting in corners
away from windows and the dog;
huddled under Jehovah's oldtime wrath,
trusting, afraid.

I huddled too, when a boy,
mindful of things they'd told me
God was bound to make me answer for.
But later I was colleged (as they said)
and learned it was not celestial ire
(Beware the infidels, my son)
but pressure systems,
colliding massive energies
that make a storm.
Well for us. . . .

Last night we drove
through suddenly warring weather.
Wind and lightning havocked,
berserked in wires, trees.
Fallen lines we could not see at first
lay in the yard when we reached home.
The hedge was burning in the rain.

Who knows but what
we might have crossed another sill,
had not our neighbors' warning
kept us from our door?
Who knows if it was heavenly design
or chance
(or knows if there's a difference, after all)
that brought us and our neighbors through—
though others died—
the archetypal dangers of the night?

I know what those
cowering true believers would have said.

Full Moon

No longer throne of a goddess to whom we pray,
no longer the bubble house of childhood's
tumbling Mother Goose man,

The emphatic moon ascends—
the brilliant challenger of rocket experts,
the white hope of communications men.

Some I love who are dead
were watchers of the moon and knew its lore;
planted seeds, trimmed their hair,

Pierced their ears for gold hoop earrings
as it waxed or waned.
It shines tonight upon their graves.

And burned in the garden of Gethsemane,
its light made holy by the dazzling tears
with which it mingled.

And spread its radiance on the exile's path
of Him who was The Glorious One,
its light made holy by His holiness.

Already a mooted goal and tomorrow perhaps
an arms base, a livid sector,
the full moon dominates the dark.

Dawnbreaker

Ablaze
with candles sconced
in weeping eyes
    of wounds,

He danced
through jeering streets
to death; oh sang
    against

The drumming
mockery God's praise.
Flames nested in
    his flesh

Fed the
fires that consume
us now, the fire that
    will save.

The Rabbi

Where I grew up, I used to see
the rabbi, dour and pale
in religion's mourner clothes,
walking to the synagogue.

Once there, did he put on
sackcloth and ashes? Wail?
He would not let me in to see
the gold menorah burning.

Mazuzah, Pesach, Chanukah—
these were timbred words I learned,
were things I knew by glimpses.
And I learned schwartze too

And schnapps, which schwartzes bought
on credit from "Jew Baby."
Tippling ironists laughed and said
he'd soon be rich as Rothschild

From their swinish Saturdays.
Hirschel and Molly and I meanwhile
divvied halveh, polly seeds,
were spies and owls and Fu Manchu.

But the synagogue became
New Calvary.
The rabbi bore my friends off
in his prayer shawl.

Belsen, Day of Liberation
(for Rosey)

Her parents and her dolls destroyed,
    her childhood foreclosed,
she watched the foreign soldiers from
    the sunlit window whose black bars

Were crooked crosses inked upon
    her pallid face. "Liebchen,
Liebchen, you should be in bed."
    But she felt ill no longer.

And because that day was a holy day
    when even the dead, it seemed,
must rise, she was allowed to stay
    and see the golden strangers who

Were Father, Brother, and her dream
    of God. Afterwards
she said, "They were so beautiful,
    and they were not afraid."

Approximations

I
In dead of winter
wept beside your open grave.
Falling snow.

II
Darkness, darkness.
I grope and falter. Flare
of a match.

III
Not sunflowers, not
roses, but rocks in patterned
sand grow here. And bloom.

IV
On the platform at
dawn, grey mailbags waiting;
a crated coffin.

Snow

Smooths and burdens,
endangers, hardens.

Erases, revises.
Extemporizes

Vistas of lunar solitude.
Builds, embellishes a mood.

The Ballad of Sue Ellen Westerfield
(for Clyde)

She grew up in bedeviled southern wilderness,
but had not been a slave, she said,
because her father wept and set her mother free.
She hardened in perilous rivertowns
and after The Surrender,
went as maid upon the tarnished Floating Palaces.
Rivermen reviled her for the rankling cold
sardonic pride
that gave a knife-edge to her comeliness.

When she was old, her back still straight,
her hair still glossy black,
she'd talk sometimes
of dangers lived through on the rivers.
But never told of him,
whose name she'd vowed she would not speak again
till after Jordan.
Oh, he was nearer nearer now
than wearisome kith and kin.
His blue eyes followed her
as she moved about her tasks upon the *Memphis Rose*.
He smiled and joshed, his voice quickening her.
She cursed the circumstance. . . .

The crazing horrors of that summer night,
the swifting flames, he fought his way to her,
the savaging panic, and helped her swim to shore.
The steamer like besieged Atlanta blazing,
the cries, the smoke and bellowing flames,
the flamelit thrashing forms in hellmouth water,
and he swimming out to them,
leaving her dazed and lost.
A woman screaming under the raddled trees—

13

Sue Ellen felt it was herself who screamed.
The moaning of the hurt, the terrified—
she held off shuddering despair
and went to comfort whom she could.
Wagons torches bells
and whimpering dusk of morning
and blankness lostness nothingness for her
until his arms had lifted her
into wild and secret dark.

How long how long was it they wandered,
loving fearing loving,
fugitives whose dangerous only hidingplace
was love?
How long was it before she knew
she could not forfeit what she was,
even for him—could not, even for him,
forswear her pride?
They kissed and said farewell at last.
He wept as had her father once.
They kissed and said farewell.
Until her dying-bed,
she cursed the circumstance.

Night, Death, Mississippi

A quavering cry. Screech-owl?
Or one of them?
The old man in his reek
and gauntness laughs—

One of them, I bet—
and turns out the kitchen lamp,
limping to the porch to listen
in the windowless night.

Be there with Boy and the rest
if I was well again.
Time was. Time was.
White robes like moonlight

In the sweetgum dark.
Unbucked that one then
and him squealing bloody Jesus
as we cut it off.

Time was. A cry?
A cry all right.
He hawks and spits,
fevered as by groinfire.

Have us a bottle,
Boy and me—
he's earned him a bottle—
when he gets home.

II

Then we beat them, he said,
beat them till our arms was tired
and the big old chains
messy and red.

O Jesus burning on the lily cross

Christ, it was better
than hunting bear
which don't know why
you want him dead.

O night, rawhead and bloodybones night

You kids fetch Paw
some water now so's he
can wash that blood
off him, she said.

O night betrayed by darkness not its own

16

"An Inference of Mexico"
(for Hank and Richard)
1. *Day of the Dead (Tehuantepec)*

The vultures hover wheel and hover
in skies intense as voyeur's gazing.

Cruciform black bells of clay
serenade Mr. and Mrs. Death
exposed in wedding clothes.

> Savage the light upon us,
> savage the light.

The graveblack vultures encircle afternoon,
transformed by steeps of flight
into dark pure images of flight.

> Such pretty girls in Juchitán, señor,
> and if one desires—

Death brings an almond sweetness
to the lips of children playing
with Jack-in-the-tomb and skulls of marzipan.

The tilting vultures glide
through causeway smoke to carrion.

In flowered shirt, androgynous,
the young man under palmleaf knives of sunlight
invites, awaits, obliquely smiles.

> Such pretty girls, señor,
> but if instead—

Barefoot Tehuanas in rhythmic jewels of gold
bear pails of marigolds upon their heads
to the returning dead.

> Flee, amigo, for the dead are angry;
> flee, lest the hands of dead men strike us down,
> and the vultures pick our bones.

17

2. Mountains

Dark as if cloven from darkness
were those mountains.

Night-angled fold on fold
they rose in mist and sunlight,

Their surging darkness
drums bells gongs imploring a god.

3. Veracruz

I

Sunday afternoon,
and couples walk the breakwater
heedless of the bickering spray.
Near the shoreward end,
Indian boys idle and fish.
A shawled brown woman
squinting against
the ricocheting brilliance
of sun and water
shades her eyes and gazes
toward the fort,
fossil of Spanish power,
looming in the harbor.

At the seaward end,
a pharos like a temple rises.
From here the shore
seen across marbling waves
is arabesque ornately green
that hides the inward-falling slum,
the stains and dirty tools of struggle;
appears a destination dreamed of,
never to be reached.

Here only the sea is real—
the barbarous multifoliate sea
with its rustling of leaves,
fire, garments, wind;
its clashing of phantasmal jewels,
its lunar thunder,
animal and human sighing.

Leap now
and cease from error.
Escape. Or shoreward turn,

accepting all—
the losses and farewells,
the long warfare with self,
with God.

The waves roar in and break
roar in and break
with granite spreeing hiss
on bronzegreen rocks below
and glistering upfling of spray.

II

Thus reality
      bedizened in the warring colors
            of a dream
parades through these
      arcades ornate with music and
            the sea.

Thus reality
      become unbearably a dream
            beckons
out of reach in flyblown streets
      of lapsing rose and purple, dying
            blue.

Thus marimba'd night
      and multifoliate sea become
            phantasmal
space, and there,
      light-years away, one farewell image
            burns and fades and burns.

20

4. Idol
(Coatlicue, Aztec goddess)

Wail of the newborn, cry of the dying,
sirenscream of agonies;
    taloned shriek, gong and cymbal of wreckage,
drumbeat of bloodblackened praise;
    soundless drumthrob of the heart wrenched
from the living breast,
    of the raw meaty heart quivering in copal
smoke its praise.

5. *Sub Specie Aeternitatis*

         High amid
gothic rocks the altar stands
that honored once
         a tippling fiercely joyous god.
         Far below,
the empty convent lifts
its cross against a dark
         invasive as the sun
         whose plangent fire
moves like feathered snakes
in trees that shade
         the cloister-garth.

         The curious
may walk the cloister now,
may enter portals barred
         to them no longer
         and wander
hidden passageways and rooms
of stone, meditating on
         such gods as they possess,
         as they have lost.

         Hollow cells
are desolate in their
tranquility
         as relic skulls.
         Arched windows there
look toward the firegreen mountain
resonant with silence of
         a conquered and
         defiant god.

6. Market

Ragged boys
lift sweets, haggle
for acid-green
and bloody gelatins.
A broken smile
dandles its weedy
cigarette
over papayas too ripe
and pyramids
of rotting oranges.
Turkeys like feather-
duster flowers
lie trussed in bunchy smother.
The barefoot cripple
foraging crawls
among rinds, orts,
chewed butts, trampled
peony droppings—
his hunger litany
and suppliant before
altars of mamey,
pineapple, mango.
Turistas pass.
Por caridad, por caridad.
Lord, how they stride
on the hard good legs
money has made them.
Ay! you creatures
who have walked
on seas of money all
your foreign lives!
Por caridad.

Odor of a dripping
carcass moans
beneath the hot
fragrance of carnations,
cool scent of lilies.
Starveling dogs
hover in the reek
of frying; ashy feet
(the twistfoot beggar laughs)
kick at them in vain.
Aloft, the Fire King's
flashing mask of tin
looks down with eyes
of sunstruck glass.

7. *Kid*
(Cuernavaca)

He is found with the homeless dogs
    that worry sidewalk cafes
where gringos in dollar bills
    deplore and sip. He has

Tricks of pathos for
    the silly foreigners
and so manages not to starve.
    Waiters strike at him and curse;

Deft and quick and accustomed,
    he dances beyond their blows,
taunts them and scampers off,
    laughing as he goes.

8. La Corrida

El toro
From the blind kingdom
where his horns are law,

Gigantically plunging and charging,
he enters the clockface labyrinth—

Man-in-beast, creature
whose guileless power is his doom.

El matador
In the heart of the maze
whose ritual pathways
goading lance, bloodflowering dart,
veronica and sword define,

The fateful one, fate's dazzler,
gleams in suit of lights,
prepares for sensual death
his moment of mocking truth.

In the fiery heart of the maze
the bullgod moves,
transfiguring death
and the wish to die.

Sol y sombra
From all we are yet cannot be
deliver, oh redeem us now.

Of all we know and do not wish
to know, purge oh purge us now.

Olé!

Upon the cross of horns
be crucified for us.

Die for us that death
may call us back to life.

Olé!

A Ballad of Remembrance

Quadroon mermaids, Afro angels, black saints
balanced upon the switchblades of that air
and sang. Tight streets unfolding to the eye
like fans of corrosion and elegiac lace
crackled with their singing: Shadow of time. Shadow of blood.

Shadow, echoed the Zulu king, dangling
from a cluster of balloons. Blood,
whined the gun-metal priestess, floating
over the courtyard where dead men diced.

What will you have? she inquired, the sallow vendeuse
of prepared tarnishes and jokes of nacre and ormolu,
what but those gleamings, oldrose graces,
manners like scented gloves? Contrived ghosts
rapped to metronome clack of lavalieres.

Contrived illuminations riding a threat
of river, masked Negroes wearing chameleon
satins gaudy now as a fortuneteller's
dream of disaster, lighted the crazy flopping
dance of love and hate among joys, rejections.

Accommodate, muttered the Zulu king,
toad on a throne of glaucous poison jewels.
Love, chimed the saints and the angels and the mermaids.
Hate, shrieked the gun-metal priestess
from her spiked bellcollar curved like a fleur-de-lis:

As well have a talon as a finger, a muzzle as a mouth,
as well have a hollow as a heart. And she pinwheeled
away in coruscations of laughter, scattering
those others before her like foil stars.

But the dance continued—now among metaphorical
doors, coffee cups floating poised
hysterias, decors of illusion; now among
mazurka dolls offering death's-heads
of cocaine roses and real violets.

Then you arrived, meditative, ironic,
richly human; and your presence was shore where I rested
released from the hoodoo of that dance, where I spoke
with my true voice again.

And therefore this is not only a ballad of remembrance
for the down-South arcane city with death
in its jaws like gold teeth and archaic cusswords;
not only a token for the troubled generous friends
held in the fists of that schizoid city like flowers,
but also, Mark Van Doren,
a poem of remembrance, a gift, a souvenir for you.

Tour 5

The road winds down through autumn hills
in blazonry of farewell scarlet
and recessional gold,
past cedar groves, through static villages
whose names are all that's left
of Choctaw, Chickasaw.

We stop a moment in a town
watched over by Confederate sentinels,
buy gas and ask directions of a rawboned man
whose eyes revile us as the enemy.

Shrill gorgon silence breathes behind
his taut civility
and in the ever-tautening air,
dark for us despite its Indian summer glow.
We drive on, following the route
of highwaymen and phantoms,

Of slaves and armies.
Children, wordless and remote,
wave at us from kindling porches.
And now the land is flat for miles,
the landscape lush, metallic, flayed,
its brightness harsh as bloodstained swords.

Gulls

In sun-whetted
      morning,
the dropped gull
      splayed
on sand,
      wind
picking at
      its feathers.

Over the headlong
      toppling
rush and leashed-back
      mica'd
fall of the sea,
      gulls
scouting and
      crying.

A Road in Kentucky

And when that ballad lady went
    to ease the lover whose life she broke,
oh surely this is the road she took,
    road all hackled through barberry fire,
through cedar and alder and sumac and thorn.

Red clay stained her flounces
    and stones cut her shoes
and the road twisted on to his loveless house
    and his cornfield dying
in the scarecrow's arms.

And when she had left her lover lying
    so stark and so stark, with the Star-of-Hope
drawn over his eyes, oh this is the road
    that lady walked in the cawing light,
so dark and so dark in the briary light.

Homage to the Empress of the Blues

Because there was a man somewhere in a candystripe silk shirt,
gracile and dangerous as a jaguar and because a woman moaned
for him in sixty-watt gloom and mourned him Faithless Love
Twotiming Love Oh Love Oh Careless Aggravating Love,

> She came out on the stage in yards of pearls, emerging like
> a favorite scenic view, flashed her golden smile and sang.

Because grey laths began somewhere to show from underneath
torn hurdygurdy lithographs of dollfaced heaven;
and because there were those who feared alarming fists of snow
on the door and those who feared the riot-squad of statistics,

> She came out on the stage in ostrich feathers, beaded satin,
> and shone that smile on us and sang.

"The Burly Fading One"

The burly fading one beside the engine,
holding a lantern in his hand,
is Uncle Jed—bullyboy
of wintered recollections now.

Coal miner, stevedore and railroad man,
oh how he brawls and loves,
a Bible over his headlong heart
and no liquor on his breath.

And when he dies, dies not in his own
well-mastered bed but in the waters
of the Johnstown flood, in wild attempt—
so sibling innuendoes all aver—

To save the jolly girl
his wife had mortally wished dead.

"Incense of the Lucky Virgin"

Incense of the Lucky Virgin,
High John the Conqueror
didn't bring him home again,
didn't get his children fed,
    get his children fed.

I prayed and what did prayer avail?
My candles held no power.
An evening came I prayed no more
and blew my candles out,
    oh blew my candles out.

Put on your Sunday ribbon-bows,
Cleola, Willie Mae;
you, Garland, go
and shine your Sunday shoes,
    make haste and shine your shoes.

They were so happy they forgot
they were hungry, daddyless.
Except Cleola maybe—she
wasn't asking, Where we going,
    Mommy, where we going?

Garland was too quick for me
(he didn't yell once as he ran);
Cleola, Willie Mae
won't be hungry any more,
    oh they'll never cry and hunger any more.

Witch Doctor

He dines alone surrounded by reflections
of himself. Then after sleep and benzedrine
descends the Cinquecento stair his magic
wrought from hypochondria of the well-
to-do and nagging deathwish of the poor;
swirls on smiling genuflections of
his liveried chauffeur into a crested
lilac limousine, the cynosure
of mousey neighbors tittering behind
Venetian blinds and half afraid of him
and half admiring his outrageous flair.

II

Meanwhile his mother, priestess in gold lamé,
precedes him to the quondam theater
now Israel Temple of the Highest Alpha,
where the bored, the sick, the alien, the tired
await euphoria. With deadly vigor
she prepares the way for mystery
and lucre. Shouts in blues-contralto, "He's
God's dictaphone of all-redeeming truth.
Oh he's the holyweight champeen who's come
to give the knockout lick to your bad luck;
say he's the holyweight champeen who's here
to deal a knockout punch to your hard luck."

III

Reposing on cushions of black leopard skin,
he telephones instructions for a long
slow drive across the park that burgeons now
with spring and sailors. Peers questingly
into the green fountainous twilight, sighs

and turns the gold-plate dial to Music For
Your Dining-Dancing Pleasure. Smoking Egyptian
cigarettes rehearses in his mind
a new device that he must use tonight.

IV

Approaching Israel Temple, mask in place,
he hears ragtime allegros of a "Song
of Zion" that becomes when he appears
a hallelujah wave for him to walk.
His mother and a rainbow-surpliced cordon
conduct him choiring to the altar-stage,
and there he kneels and seems to pray before
a lighted Jesus painted sealskin-brown.
Then with a glittering flourish he arises,
turns, gracefully extends his draperied arms:
"Israelites, true Jews, O found lost tribe
of Israel, receive my blessing now.
Selah, selah." He feels them yearn toward him
as toward a lover, exults before the image
of himself their trust gives back. Stands as though
in meditation, letting their eyes caress
his garments jewelled and chatoyant, cut
to fall, to flow from his tall figure
dramatically just so. Then all at once
he sways, quivers, gesticulates as if
to ward off blows or kisses, and when he speaks
again he utters wildering vocables,
hypnotic no-words planned (and never failing)
to enmesh his flock in theopathic tension.
Cries of eudaemonic pain attest
his artistry. Behind the mask he smiles.
And now in subtly altering light he chants

and sinuously trembles, chants and trembles
while convulsive energies of eager faith
surcharge the theater with power of
their own, a power he has counted on
and for a space allows to carry him.
Dishevelled antiphons proclaim the moment
his followers all day have hungered for,
but which is his alone.
He signals: tambourines begin, frenetic
drumbeat and glissando. He dances from the altar,
robes hissing, flaring, shimmering; down aisles
where mantled guardsmen intercept wild hands
that arduously strain to clutch his vestments,
he dances, dances, ensorcelled and aloof,
the fervid juba of God as lover, healer,
conjurer. And of himself as God.

Mourning Poem for the Queen of Sunday

Lord's lost Him His mockingbird,
His fancy warbler;
Satan sweet-talked her,
four bullets hushed her.
Who would have thought
she'd end that way?

Four bullets hushed her. And the world a-clang with evil.
Who's going to make old hardened sinner men tremble now
and the righteous rock?
Oh who and oh who will sing Jesus down
to help with struggling and doing without and being colored
all through blue Monday?
Till way next Sunday?

All those angels
in their cretonne clouds and finery
the true believer saw
when she rared back her head and sang,
all those angels are surely weeping.
Who would have thought
she'd end that way?

Four holes in her heart. The gold works wrecked.
But she looks so natural in her big bronze coffin
among the Broken Hearts and Gates-Ajar,
it's as if any moment she'd lift her head
from its pillow of chill gardenias
and turn this quiet into shouting Sunday
and make folks forget what she did on Monday.

Oh, Satan sweet-talked her,
and four bullets hushed her.
Lord's lost Him His diva,
His fancy warbler's gone.
Who would have thought,
who would have thought she'd end that way?

"Summertime and the Living . . ."

Nobody planted roses, he recalls,
but sunflowers gangled there sometimes,
tough-stalked and bold
and like the vivid children there unplanned.
There circus-poster horses curveted
in trees of heaven
above the quarrels and shattered glass,
and he was bareback rider of them all.

No roses there in summer—
oh, never roses except when people died—
and no vacations for his elders,
so harshened after each unrelenting day
that they were shouting-angry.
But summer was, they said, the poor folks' time
of year. And he remembers
how they would sit on broken steps amid

The fevered tossings of the dusk, the dark,
wafting hearsay with funeral-parlor fans
or making evening solemn by
their quietness. Feels their Mosaic eyes
upon him, though the florist roses
that only sorrow could afford
long since have bidden them Godspeed.
Oh, summer summer summertime—

Then grim street preachers shook
their tambourines and Bibles in the face
of tolerant wickedness;
then Elks parades and big splendiferous
Jack Johnson in his diamond limousine
set the ghetto burgeoning
with fantasies
of Ethiopia spreading her gorgeous wings.

The Whipping

The old woman across the way
    is whipping the boy again
and shouting to the neighborhood
    her goodness and his wrongs.

Wildly he crashes through elephant ears,
    pleads in dusty zinnias,
while she in spite of crippling fat
    pursues and corners him.

She strikes and strikes the shrilly circling
    boy till the stick breaks
in her hand. His tears are rainy weather
    to woundlike memories:

My head gripped in bony vise
    of knees, the writhing struggle
to wrench free, the blows, the fear
    worse than blows that hateful

Words could bring, the face that I
    no longer knew or loved . . . .
Well, it is over now, it is over,
    and the boy sobs in his room,

And the woman leans muttering against
    a tree, exhausted, purged—
avenged in part for lifelong hidings
    she has had to bear.

Those Winter Sundays

Sundays too my father got up early
and put his clothes on in the blueblack cold,
then with cracked hands that ached
from labor in the weekday weather made
banked fires blaze. No one ever thanked him.

I'd wake and hear the cold splintering, breaking.
When the rooms were warm, he'd call,
and slowly I would rise and dress,
fearing the chronic angers of that house,

Speaking indifferently to him,
who had driven out the cold
and polished my good shoes as well.
What did I know, what did I know
of love's austere and lonely offices?

The Web

My hand by chance
brushed and tore
a spider's web;

The spider dangled,
aerialist hanging
by a thread,

Then fled the ruin,
fit snare for nothing
now but my

Embittered thoughts
of a web
more intricate,

More fragile—and
the stronger for
its fragileness.

Its iron gossamer
withstands the blows
that would destroy.

Caught in that filmy
trap, who shall
contrive escape?

The Wheel

Gentle and smiling as before,
he stroked the leopard purring by his chair
and whispered silkily to me.
And though I knew he lied,
lied with every flicker of
his jewelled hands,

I listened and believed,
persuaded as before
by what he seemed to say
yet did not say.
And when, face close to mine,
he murmured that equivocal command,

I went to do his bidding as before.
And so once more,
the useless errand bitterly accomplished,
I crouch in the foulness of a ditch;
like traitor, thief or murderer hide
and curse the moon and fear the rising of the sun.

Perseus

Her sleeping head with its great gelid mass
    of serpents torpidly astir
burned into the mirroring shield—
    a scathing image dire
as hated truth the mind accepts at last
    and festers on.
I struck. The shield flashed bare.

Yet even as I lifted up the head
    and started from that place
of gazing silences and terrored stone,
    I thirsted to destroy.
None could have passed me then—
    no garland-bearing girl, no priest
or staring boy—and lived.

Theme and Variation
(for Erma)

I

Fossil, fuchsia, mantis, man,
fire and water, earth and air—
all things alter even as I behold,
all things alter, the stranger said.

Alter, become a something more,
a something less. Are the revelling shadows
of a changing permanence. Are, are not
and same and other, the stranger said.

II

I sense, he said, the lurking rush, the sly
transience flickering at the edge of things.
I've spied from the corner of my eye
upon the striptease of reality.

There is, there is, he said, an imminence
that turns to curiosa all I know;
that changes light to rainbow darkness
wherein God waylays us and empowers.

"From the Corpse Woodpiles, from the Ashes"

From the corpse woodpiles, from the ashes
and staring pits of Dachau,
Buchenwald they come—

O David, Hirschel, Eva,
cops and robbers with me once,
their faces are like yours—

From Johannesburg, from Seoul.
Their struggles are all horizons.
Their deaths encircle me.

Through target streets I run,
in light part nightmare
and part vision fleeing

What I cannot flee, and reach
that cold cloacal cell
where He, who is man beatified

And Godly mystery,
lies chained, His pain
our anguish and our anodyne.

Bahá'u'lláh in the Garden of Ridwan

Agonies confirm His hour,
    and swords like compass-needles turn
        toward His heart.

The midnight air is forested
    with presences that shelter Him
        and sheltering praise

The auroral darkness which is God
    and sing the word made flesh again
        in Him,

Eternal exile whose return
    epiphanies repeatedly
        foretell.

He watches in a borrowed garden,
    prays. And sleepers toss upon
        their armored beds,

Half-roused by golden knocking at
    the doors of consciousness. Energies
        like angels dance

Glorias of recognition.
    Within the rock the undiscovered suns
        release their light.

Middle Passage

Jesús, Estrella, Esperanza, Mercy:

> Sails flashing to the wind like weapons,
> sharks following the moans the fever and the dying;
> horror the corposant and compass rose.

Middle Passage:
> voyage through death
>> to life upon these shores.

> "10 April 1800—
> Blacks rebellious. Crew uneasy. Our linguist says
> their moaning is a prayer for death,
> ours and their own. Some try to starve themselves.
> Lost three this morning leaped with crazy laughter
> to the waiting sharks, sang as they went under."

Desire, Adventure, Tartar, Ann:

> Standing to America, bringing home
> black gold, black ivory, black seed.

>> *Deep in the festering hold thy father lies,*
>> *of his bones New England pews are made,*
>> *those are altar lights that were his eyes.*

Jesus   Saviour   Pilot   Me
Over   Life's   Tempestuous   Sea

We pray that Thou wilt grant, O Lord,
safe passage to our vessels bringing
heathen souls unto Thy chastening.

Jesus   Saviour

"8 bells. I cannot sleep, for I am sick
with fear, but writing eases fear a little
since still my eyes can see these words take shape
upon the page & so I write, as one
would turn to exorcism. 4 days scudding,
but now the sea is calm again. Misfortune
follows in our wake like sharks (our grinning
tutelary gods). Which one of us
has killed an albatross? A plague among
our blacks—Ophthalmia: blindness—& we
have jettisoned the blind to no avail.
It spreads, the terrifying sickness spreads.
Its claws have scratched sight from the Capt.'s eyes
& there is blindness in the fo'c'sle
& we must sail 3 weeks before we come
to port."

> *What port awaits us, Davy Jones'*
> *or home? I've heard of slavers drifting, drifting,*
> *playthings of wind and storm and chance, their crews*
> *gone blind, the jungle hatred*
> *crawling up on deck.*

Thou   Who   Walked   On   Galilee

> "Deponent further sayeth *The Bella J*
> left the Guinea Coast
> with cargo of five hundred blacks and odd
> for the barracoons of Florida:
>
> "That there was hardly room 'tween-decks for half
> the sweltering cattle stowed spoon-fashion there;
> that some went mad of thirst and tore their flesh
> and sucked the blood:

49

"That Crew and Captain lusted with the comeliest
of the savage girls kept naked in the cabins;
that there was one they called The Guinea Rose
and they cast lots and fought to lie with her:

"That when the Bo's'n piped all hands, the flames
spreading from starboard already were beyond
control, the negroes howling and their chains
entangled with the flames:

"That the burning blacks could not be reached,
that the Crew abandoned ship,
leaving their shrieking negresses behind,
that the Captain perished drunken with the wenches:

"Further Deponent sayeth not."

Pilot   Oh   Pilot   Me

II

Aye, lad, and I have seen those factories,
Gambia, Rio Pongo, Calabar;
have watched the artful mongos baiting traps
of war wherein the victor and the vanquished

Were caught as prizes for our barracoons.
Have seen the nigger kings whose vanity
and greed turned wild black hides of Fellatah,
Mandingo, Ibo, Kru to gold for us.

And there was one—King Anthracite we named him—
fetish face beneath French parasols
of brass and orange velvet, impudent mouth
whose cups were carven skulls of enemies:

50

He'd honor us with drum and feast and conjo
and palm-oil-glistening wenches deft in love,
and for tin crowns that shone with paste,
red calico and German-silver trinkets

Would have the drums talk war and send
his warriors to burn the sleeping villages
and kill the sick and old and lead the young
in coffles to our factories.

Twenty years a trader, twenty years,
for there was wealth aplenty to be harvested
from those black fields, and I'd be trading still
but for the fevers melting down my bones.

III

Shuttles in the rocking loom of history,
the dark ships move, the dark ships move,
their bright ironical names
like jests of kindness on a murderer's mouth;
plough through thrashing glister toward
fata morgana's lucent melting shore,
weave toward New World littorals that are
mirage and myth and actual shore.

Voyage through death,
                    voyage whose chartings are unlove.

A charnel stench, effluvium of living death
spreads outward from the hold,
where the living and the dead, the horribly dying,
lie interlocked, lie foul with blood and excrement.

> *Deep in the festering hold thy father lies,*
> *the corpse of mercy rots with him,*
> *rats eat love's rotten gelid eyes.*

But, oh, the living look at you
with human eyes whose suffering accuses you,
whose hatred reaches through the swill of dark
to strike you like a leper's claw.

You cannot stare that hatred down
or chain the fear that stalks the watches
and breathes on you its fetid scorching breath;
cannot kill the deep immortal human wish,
the timeless will.

"But for the storm that flung up barriers
of wind and wave, *The Amistad*, señores,
would have reached the port of Príncipe in two,
three days at most; but for the storm we should
have been prepared for what befell.
Swift as the puma's leap it came. There was
that interval of moonless calm filled only
with the water's and the rigging's usual sounds,
then sudden movement, blows and snarling cries
and they had fallen on us with machete
and marlinspike. It was as though the very
air, the night itself were striking us.
Exhausted by the rigors of the storm,
we were no match for them. Our men went down
before the murderous Africans. Our loyal
Celestino ran from below with gun
and lantern and I saw, before the cane-
knife's wounding flash, Cinquez,
that surly brute who calls himself a prince,
directing, urging on the ghastly work.
He hacked the poor mulatto down, and then
he turned on me. The decks were slippery

when daylight finally came. It sickens me
to think of what I saw, of how these apes
threw overboard the butchered bodies of
our men, true Christians all, like so much jetsam.
Enough, enough. The rest is quickly told:
Cinquez was forced to spare the two of us
you see to steer the ship to Africa,
and we like phantoms doomed to rove the sea
voyaged east by day and west by night,
deceiving them, hoping for rescue,
prisoners on our own vessel, till
at length we drifted to the shores of this
your land, America, where we were freed
from our unspeakable misery. Now we
demand, good sirs, the extradition of
Cinquez and his accomplices to La
Havana. And it distresses us to know
there are so many here who seem inclined
to justify the mutiny of these blacks.
We find it paradoxical indeed
that you whose wealth, whose tree of liberty
are rooted in the labor of your slaves
should suffer the august John Quincy Adams
to speak with so much passion of the right
of chattel slaves to kill their lawful masters
and with his Roman rhetoric weave a hero's
garland for Cinquez. I tell you that
we are determined to return to Cuba
with our slaves and there see justice done. Cinquez—
or let us say 'the Prince'—Cinquez shall die."

The deep immortal human wish,
the timeless will:

Cinquez its deathless primaveral image,
life that transfigures many lives.

Voyage through death
                    to life upon these shores.

O Daedalus, Fly Away Home
(For Maia and Julie)

Drifting night in the Georgia pines,
coonskin drum and jubilee banjo.
   Pretty Malinda, dance with me.

Night is juba, night is conjo.
   Pretty Malinda, dance with me.

Night is an African juju man
weaving a wish and a weariness together
   to make two wings.

   O fly away home fly away

Do you remember Africa?

   O cleave the air fly away home

My gran, he flew back to Africa,
just spread his arms and
   flew away home.

Drifting night in the windy pines;
night is a laughing, night is a longing.
   Pretty Malinda, come to me.

Night is a mourning juju man
weaving a wish and a weariness together
   to make two wings.

   O fly away home fly away

The Ballad of Nat Turner

Then fled, O brethren, the wicked juba
        and wandered wandered far
from curfew joys in the Dismal's night.
        Fool of St. Elmo's fire

In scary night I wandered, praying,
        Lord God my harshener,
speak to me now or let me die;
        speak, Lord, to this mourner.

And came at length to livid trees
        where Ibo warriors
hung shadowless, turning in wind
        that moaned like Africa,

Their belltongue bodies dead, their eyes
        alive with the anger deep
in my own heart. Is this the sign,
        the sign forepromised me?

The spirits vanished. Afraid and lonely
        I wandered on in blackness.
Speak to me now or let me die.
        Die, whispered the blackness.

And wild things gasped and scuffled in
        the night; seething shapes
of evil frolicked upon the air.
        I reeled with fear, I prayed.

Sudden brightness clove the preying
        darkness, brightness that was
itself a golden darkness, brightness
        so bright that it was darkness.

And there were angels, their faces hidden
    from me, angels at war
with one another, angels in dazzling
    combat. And oh the splendor,

The fearful splendor of that warring.
    Hide me, I cried to rock and bramble.
Hide me, the rock, the bramble cried. . . .
    How tell you of that holy battle?

The shock of wing on wing and sword
    on sword was the tumult of
a taken city burning. I cannot
    say how long they strove,

For the wheel in a turning wheel which is time
    in eternity had ceased
its whirling, and owl and moccasin,
    panther and nameless beast

And I were held like creatures fixed
    in flaming, in fiery amber.
But I saw I saw oh many of
    those mighty beings waver,

Waver and fall, go streaking down
    into swamp water, and the water
hissed and steamed and bubbled and locked
    shuddering shuddering over

The fallen and soon was motionless.
    Then that massive light
began a-folding slowly in
    upon itself, and I

Beheld the conqueror faces and, lo,
 they were like mine, I saw
they were like mine and in joy and terror
 wept, praising praising Jehovah.

Oh praised my honer, harshener
 till a sleep came over me,
a sleep heavy as death. And when
 I awoke at last free

And purified, I rose and prayed
 and returned after a time
to the blazing fields, to the humbleness.
 And bided my time.

Runagate Runagate

Runs falls rises stumbles on from darkness into darkness
and the darkness thicketed with shapes of terror
and the hunters pursuing and the hounds pursuing
and the night cold and the night long and the river
to cross and the jack-muh-lanterns beckoning beckoning
and blackness ahead and when shall I reach that somewhere
morning and keep on going and never turn back and keep on going
      Runagate
          Runagate
             Runagate

Many thousands rise and go
many thousands crossing over

                  O mythic North
            O star-shaped yonder Bible city

Some go weeping and some rejoicing
some in coffins and some in carriages
some in silks and some in shackles

      Rise and go or fare you well

No more auction block for me
no more driver's lash for me

      If you see my Pompey, 30 yrs of age,
      new breeches, plain stockings, negro shoes;
      if you see my Anna, likely young mulatto
      branded E on the right cheek, R on the left,
      catch them if you can and notify subscriber.
      Catch them if you can, but it won't be easy.
      They'll dart underground when you try to catch them,
      plunge into quicksand, whirlpools, mazes,
      turn into scorpions when you try to catch them.

And before I'll be a slave
I'll be buried in my grave

North star and bonanza gold
I'm bound for the freedom, freedom-bound
and oh Susyanna don't you cry for me

Runagate

Runagate

II.
Rises from their anguish and their power,

Harriet Tubman,

woman of earth, whipscarred,
a summoning, a shining

Mean to be free

And this was the way of it, brethren brethren,
way we journeyed from Can't to Can.
Moon so bright and no place to hide,
the cry up and the patterollers riding,
hound dogs belling in bladed air.
And fear starts a-murbling, Never make it,
we'll never make it. *Hush that now,*
and she's turned upon us, levelled pistol
glinting in the moonlight:
Dead folks can't jaybird-talk, she says;
you keep on going now or die, she says.

Wanted   Harriet Tubman   alias The General
alias Moses   Stealer of Slaves

In league with Garrison   Alcott   Emerson
Garrett   Douglass   Thoreau   John Brown

Armed and known to be Dangerous

Wanted   Reward   Dead or Alive

    Tell me, Ezekiel, oh tell me do you see
    mailed Jehovah coming to deliver me?

Hoot-owl calling in the ghosted air,
five times calling to the hants in the air.
Shadow of a face in the scary leaves,
shadow of a voice in the talking leaves:

    Come ride-a my train

    Oh that train, ghost-story train
    through swamp and savanna movering movering,
    over trestles of dew, through caves of the wish,
    Midnight Special on a sabre track movering movering,
    first stop Mercy and the last Hallelujah.

    Come ride-a my train

    Mean mean mean to be free.

Frederick Douglass

When it is finally ours, this freedom, this liberty, this beautiful
and terrible thing, needful to man as air,
usable as earth; when it belongs at last to all,
when it is truly instinct, brain matter, diastole, systole,
reflex action; when it is finally won; when it is more
than the gaudy mumbo jumbo of politicians:
this man, this Douglass, this former slave, this Negro
beaten to his knees, exiled, visioning a world
where none is lonely, none hunted, alien,
this man, superb in love and logic, this man
shall be remembered. Oh, not with statues' rhetoric,
not with legends and poems and wreaths of bronze alone,
but with the lives grown out of his life, the lives
fleshing his dream of the beautiful, needful thing.

Words in the Mourning Time (1970)

&

For Marie Alice Hanson
and Louis Martin
with gratitude

Sphinx

If he could solve the riddle,
she would not leap
    from those gaunt rocks to her death,
but devour him instead.

It pleasures her to hold
him captive there—
    to keep him in the reach of her
blood-matted paws.

It is your fate, she has often
said, to endure
    my riddling. Your fate to live
at the mercy of my

conundrum, which, in truth,
is only a kind
    of psychic joke. No, you shall
not leave this place.

(Consider anyway the view from
here.) In time,
    you will come to regard my questioning
with a certain pained

amusement; in time, get so
you would hardly find
    it possible to live without
my joke and me.

The Dream
(1863)

That evening Sinda thought she heard the drums
and hobbled from her cabin to the yard.
The quarters now were lonely-still in willow dusk
after the morning's ragged jubilo,
when laughing crying singing the folks went off
with Marse Lincum's soldier boys.
But Sinda hiding would not follow them: those
Buckras with their ornery
funning, cussed commands, oh they were not were not
the hosts the dream had promised her.

and hope when these few lines reaches your hand they
will fine you well. I am tired some but it is war you know
and ole jeff Davis muss be ketch an hung to a sour apple
tree like it says in the song   I seen some akshun but
that is what i listed for not to see the sights ha ha More of
our peeples coming every day. the Kernul calls them
contrybans and has them work aroun the Camp and
learning to be soljurs. How is the wether home. Its warm
this evening but theres been lots of rain

How many times that dream had come to her—
more vision than a dream—
the great big soldiers marching out of gunburst,
their faces those of Cal and Joe
and Charlie sold to the ricefields oh sold away
a-many and a-many a long year ago.
Fevered, gasping, Sinda listened, knew this was
the ending of her dream and prayed
that death, grown fretful and impatient, nagging her,
would wait a little longer, would let her see.

66

and we been marching sleeping too in cold rain and
mirey mud a heap a times. Tell Mama Thanks for The
Bible an not worry so. Did brother fix the roof yet like
he promised? this mus of been a real nice place befor the
fighting uglied it all up the judas trees is blosommed out
so pretty same as if this hurt and truble wasnt going on.
Almos like somthing you mite dream about i take it for
a sign The Lord remembers Us Theres talk we will be
moving into Battle very soon agin

Trembling tottering Hep me Jesus Sinda crossed
the wavering yard, reached
    a redbud tree in bloom, could go no farther, clung
to the bole and clinging fell
    to her knees. She tried to stand, could not so much
as lift her head, tried to hold
    the bannering sounds, heard only the whipoorwills
in tenuous moonlight; struggled to rise
    and make her way to the road to welcome Joe and Cal
and Charlie, fought with brittle strength to rise.

So pray for me that if the Bullit with my name rote on
it get me it will not get me in retreet i do not think them
kine of thots so much no need in Dying till you die I all
ways figger, course if the hardtack and the bullybeef do
not kill me nuthing can i guess. Tell Joe I hav shure
seen me some ficety gals down here in Dixieland & i
mite jus go ahead an jump over the broomstick with one
and bring her home, well I muss close with Love to all
& hope to see you soon Yrs Cal

" 'Mystery Boy' Looks for Kin in Nashville"

Puzzle faces in the dying elms
promise him treats if he will stay.
Sometimes they hiss and spit at him
like varmints caught
in a thicket of butterflies.

A black doll,
one disremembered time,
came floating down to him
through mimosa's fancywork leaves and blooms
to be his hidden bride.

From the road beyond the creepered walls
they call to him now and then,
and he'll take off in spite of the angry trees,
hearing like the loudening of his heart
the name he never can he never can repeat.

And when he gets to where the voices were—
Don't cry, his dollbaby wife implores;
I know where they are, don't cry.
We'll go and find them, we'll go
and ask them for your name again.

The Broken Dark

Sleepless, I stare
from the dark hospital room
at shadows of a flower and its leaves
the nightlight fixes like a blotto
on the corridor wall. Shadow-plays
of Bali—demons move to the left,
gods, in their frangipani crowns
and gold, to the right.
Ah and my life
in the shadow of God's laser light—
shadow of deformed homunculus?
A fool's errand given by fools.
Son, go fetch a pint of pigeon's milk
from the drugstore and be quick.
Demons on the left. Death on either side,
the Rabbi said, the way of life between.
That groaning. Man with his belly slashed,
two-timing lover. Dying?
The nightnurse rustles by.
Struggles in the pit. I have come back
to tell thee of struggles in the pit.
Perhaps is dying.
Free of pain, my own death still
a theorem to be proved.
Alláh'u'Abhá. O Healing Spirit,
Thy nearness our forgiving cure.

The Mirages

Exhaustion among rocks
    in rockfall sun;

    thirst, and thick
water to drink,

    the stranger said.

And the mirages, the
    mirages—

    I knew what they were
yet often

changed my course
    and followed them.

    Less lonely, less
lonely then,

    the stranger said.

Soledad
(And I, I am no longer of that world)

Naked, he lies in the blinded room
chainsmoking, cradled by drugs, by jazz
as never by any lover's cradling flesh.

Miles Davis coolly blows for him:
O pena negra, sensual Flamenco blues;
the red clay foxfire voice of Lady Day

(lady of the pure black magnolias)
sobsings her sorrow and loss and fare you well,
dryweeps the pain his treacherous jailers

have released him from for a while.
His fears and his unfinished self
await him down in the anywhere streets.

He hides on the dark side of the moon,
takes refuge in a stained-glass cell,
flies to a clockless country of crystal.

Only the ghost of Lady Day knows where
he is. Only the music. And he swings
oh swings: beyond complete immortal now.

Aunt Jemima of the Ocean Waves

I

Enacting someone's notion of themselves
(and me), The One And Only Aunt Jemima
and Kokimo The Dixie Dancing Fool
do a bally for the freak show.

I watch a moment, then move on,
pondering the logic that makes of them
(and me) confederates
of The Spider Girl, The Snake-skinned Man. . . .

Poor devils have to live somehow.

I cross the boardwalk to the beach,
lie in the sand and gaze beyond
the clutter at the sea.

Trouble you for a light?
I turn as Aunt Jemima settles down
beside me, her blue-rinsed hair
without the red bandanna now.

I hold the lighter to her cigarette.
Much obliged. Unmindful (perhaps)
of my embarrassment, she looks
at me and smiles: You sure

do favor a friend I used to have.
Guess that's why I bothered you
for a light. So much like him that I—
She pauses, watching white horses rush

to the shore. Way them big old waves
come slamming whopping in,
sometimes it's like they mean to smash
this no-good world to hell.

Well, it could happen. A book I read—
Crossed that very ocean years ago.
London, Paris, Rome,
Constantinople too—I've seen them all.

Back when they billed me everywhere
as the Sepia High Stepper.
Crowned heads applauded me.
Years before your time. Years and years.

I wore me plenty diamonds then,
and counts or dukes or whatever they were
would fill my dressing room
with the costliest flowers. But of course

there was this one you resemble so.
Get me? The sweetest gentleman.
Dead before his time. Killed in the war
to save the world for another war.

High-stepping days for me
were over after that. Still I'm not one
to let grief idle me for long.
I went out with a mental act—

mind-reading—Mysteria From
The Mystic East—veils and beads
and telling suckers how to get
stolen rings and sweethearts back.

One night he was standing by my bed,
seen him plain as I see you,
and warned me without a single word:
Baby, quit playing with spiritual stuff.

So here I am, so here I am,
fake mammy to God's mistakes.
And that's the beauty part,
I mean, ain't that the beauty part.

She laughs, but I do not, knowing what
her laughter shields. And mocks.
I light another cigarette for her.
She smokes, not saying any more.

Scream of children in the surf,
adagios of sun and flashing foam,
the sexual glitter, oppressive fun. . . .
An antique etching comes to mind:

"The Sable Venus" naked on
a baroque Cellini shell—voluptuous
imago floating in the wake
of slave-ships on fantastic seas.

Jemima sighs, Reckon I'd best
be getting back. I help her up.
Don't you take no wooden nickels, hear?
Tin dimes neither. So long, pal.

Locus
(for Ralph)

Here redbuds like momentary trees
     of an illusionist;
here Cherokee rose, acacia, and mimosa;
here magnolias—totemic flowers
     wreathing legends of this place.
Here violent metamorphosis,
     with every blossom turning
deadly and memorial soldiers,
their sabres drawn, charging
     firewood shacks,
apartheid streets. Here wound-red earth
     and blinding cottonfields,
rock hills where sachems counseled,
where scouts gazed stealthily
     upon the glittering death march
of De Soto through Indian wilderness.
     Here mockingbird and
cottonmouth, fury of rivers.
Here swamp and trace and bayou
     where the runagate hid,
the devil with Spanish pistols rode.
     Here spareness, rankness, harsh
brilliances; beauty of what's hardbitten,
knotted, stinted, flourishing
     in despite, on thorny meagerness
thriving, twisting into grace.
     Here symbol houses
where the brutal dream lives out its lengthy
dying. Here the past, adored and
     unforgiven. Here the past—
soulscape, Old Testament battleground
of warring shades whose weapons kill.

On Lookout Mountain

I listen for the sounds of cannon, cries
vibrating still upon the air,
timeless echoes in echoic time—
imagine how they circle out and out

concentric with Kilroy's cries,
as beyond the tangent calm
of this midcentury morning he burns
or freezes in the warfare of our peace.

I gaze through layered light,
think of the death-for-foothold inching climb
of Union soldiers struggling up
the crackling mountainside.

And here where Sunday alpinists
pick views and souvenirs,
here daring choices stained
the clouds with dubious victory.

A world away, yet nearer than our hope
or our belief, the scions of that fighting climb
endless hills of war, amid war's peaks
and valleys broken, scattered fall.

Have done, have done. Behold how bright
upon the mountain the gadget feet
of trivia shine.
Oh, hear the stuffed gold eagle sing.

Kodachromes of the Island

1

Halfnaked children
met us singing for coins
at the swaybacked jetty.

Gold brooms had swept
the mist away, and
the island air was clear.

Parrot and zinnia
colors teemed
in thronging sunlight.

A young beggar greeted us
Dios se lo pague
with fingerless hands.

II
Out on the yellow
as pollen or sulphur
lake Indian fishermen,

naked torsos oiled with
sunlight, were casting
their mariposas.

On the landing, women
were cleaning a catch and
tossing the guts to

squealing piglets. A tawny
butterfly drunkenly circled
then lighted on offal.

III

Black turkeys children
dogs foraged and played
under drying fishnets.

Vendors urged laquerwork
and glazed angels
with candles between their wings.

Alien, at home—as always
everywhere—I roamed
the cobbled island,

and thought of Yeats,
his passionate search for
a theme. Sought mine.

Zeus over Redeye
(The Redstone Arsenal)

Enclave where new mythologies
of power come to birth—
where coralled energy and power breed
like prized man-eating animals.
Like dragon, hydra, basilisk.

Radar corollas and Holland tulips
the colors of Easter eggs
form vistas for the ironist.
Where elm, ailanthus, redbud grew
parabola and gantry rise.

In soaring stasis rocket missiles loom,
the cherished weapons named for Nike
(O headless armless Victory),
for Zeus, Apollo, Hercules—
eponyms of redeyed fury
greater, lesser than their own.

Ignorant outlander, mere civilian,
not sure always of what it is
I see, I walk with you among
these totems of our fire-breathing age,
question and question you,

who are at home in terra guarded like
a sacred phallic grove.
Your partial answers reassure
me less than they appall.
I feel as though invisible fuses were

burning all around us burning all
around us. Heat-quiverings twitch
danger's hypersensitive skin.
The very sunlight here seems flammable.
And shadows give
us no relieving shade.

Unidentified Flying Object

It's true Mattie Lee
has clean disappeared.
And shouldn't we notify
the sheriff? No use, Will
insists, no earthly use.

He was sleeping one off
under the trees that night,
he claims, and woke up when
the space-ship
landed—a silvery dome

with gassy-green and red-
hot-looking lights like eyes
that stared blinked stared.
Says he hid himself
in the bushes and watched,

shaking. Pretty soon
a hatch slides open, a ramp
glides forward like
a glowing tongue poked out.
And who or what is it

silently present there?
Same as if Will's
trying to peer through webs
and bars of gauzy glare
screening, distorting a shape

he sees yet cannot see.
But crazier than that
was when Mattie Lee
came running from her house
toward the thing.

She's wearing her sunflower hat
and the dress the lady she cooked
for gave her, and it's like
she's late for work the way
she scurries up the ramp.

And it seems to Will
that in its queer
shining, plain Mattie Lee's
transformed—is every teasing brown
he's ever wanted, never had.

He's fixing to shout, Come back,
Mattie Lee, come back;
but a heavy hand is over his mouth
when he hears her laugh
as she steps inside

without even a goodbye glance
around. The next Will knew,
the UFO rose in the air—
no blastoff roar, no flame,
he says—hung in the dark,

hovered, shimmered,
its eyes pulsing, then whirred
spiraling into the sky,
vanished as though
it had never been.

Will's tale anyhow.
All I'm certain of
is Mattie Lee's
nowhere to be found
and must have gone

off in a hurry. Left her doors
unlocked and the radio on
and a roast in the oven. Strange.
As for Will, he's a changed man,
not drinking nowadays and sad.

Mattie Lee's friends—
she's got no kinfolks, lived
alone—are worried, swear
Will was craving her
and she held herself too good

for him, being head of Mount
Nebo's usher board and such.
And some are hinting what I,
for one—well, never mind.
The talk is getting mean.

El-Hajj Malik El-Shabazz

(Malcolm X)
O masks and metamorphoses of Ahab, Native Son

I

The icy evil that struck his father down
and ravished his mother into madness
trapped him in violence of a punished self
struggling to break free.

As Home Boy, as Dee-troit Red,
he fled his name, became the quarry of
his own obsessed pursuit.

He conked his hair and Lindy-hopped,
zoot-suited jiver, swinging those chicks
in the hot rose and reefer glow.

His injured childhood bullied him.
He skirmished in the Upas trees
and cannibal flowers of the American Dream—

but could not hurt the enemy
powered against him there.

II

Sometimes the dark that gave his life
its cold satanic sheen would shift
a little, and he saw himself
floodlit and eloquent;

yet how could he, "Satan" in The Hole,
guess what the waking dream foretold?

Then false dawn of vision came;
he fell upon his face before
a racist Allah pledged to wrest him from
the hellward-thrusting hands of Calvin's Christ—

to free him and his kind
from Yakub's white-faced treachery.
He rose redeemed from all but prideful anger,

though adulterate attars could not cleanse
him of the odors of the pit.

III
Asalam alaikum!

He X'd his name, became his people's anger,
exhorted them to vengeance for their past;
rebuked, admonished them,

their scourger who
would shame them, drive them from
the lush ice gardens of their servitude.

Asalam alaikum!

Rejecting Ahab, he was of Ahab's tribe.
"Strike through the mask!"

IV

Time. "The martyr's time," he said.
Time and the karate killer,
knifer, gunman. Time that brought
ironic trophies as his faith

twined sparking round the bole,
the fruit of neo-Islam.
"The martyr's time."

But first, the ebb time pilgrimage
toward revelation, hejira to
his final metamorphosis;

Labbayk! Labbayk!

He fell upon his face before
Allah the raceless in whose blazing Oneness all
were one. He rose renewed renamed, became
much more than there was time for him to be.

Words in the Mourning Time

I

For King, for Robert Kennedy,
destroyed by those they could not save,
for King for Kennedy I mourn.
And for America, self-destructive, self-betrayed.

I grieve. Yet know the vanity
of grief—through power of
The Blessed Exile's
transilluminating word

aware of how these deaths, how all
the agonies of our deathbed childbed age
are process, major means whereby,
oh dreadfully, our humanness must be achieved.

II
Killing people to save, to free them?
With napalm lighting routes to the future?

III

He comes to my table in his hungry wounds
and his hunger. The flamed-out eyes,
their sockets dripping. The nightmare mouth.

He snatches food from my plate, raw
fingers bleeding, seizes my glass
and drinks, leaving flesh-fragments on its rim.

IV
Vietnam   bloodclotted name in my consciousness
recurring and recurring
like the obsessive thought many midnights
now of my own dying

Vietnam   and I think of the villages
mistakenly burning   the schoolrooms devouring
their children   and I think of those who
were my students
                    brutalized   killing
wasted by horror
in ultimate loneliness
dying
            Vietnam Vietnam

V

Oh, what a world we make,
oppressor and oppressed.

Our world—
this violent ghetto, slum
of the spirit raging against itself.

We hate kill destroy
in the name of human good
our killing and our hate destroy.

VI

Lord Riot
       naked
           in flaming clothes
cannibal ruler
         of anger's
              carousals
     sing hey nonny no
terror
    his tribute
          shriek of bloody glass
his praise
    sing wrathful sing vengeful
       sing hey nonny no
gigantic
    and laughing
           sniper on tower
I hate
   I destroy
      I am I am
    sing hey nonny no
    sing burn baby burn

VII
voice in the wilderness

Know that love has chosen you
to live his crucial purposes.
Know that love has chosen you.

And will not pamper you nor spare;
demands obedience to all
the rigorous laws of risk,
does not pamper, will not spare.

Oh, master now love's instruments—
complex and not for the fearful,
simple and not for the foolish.
Master now love's instruments.

I who love you tell you this,
even as the pitiful killer waits for me,
I who love you tell you this.

VIII
Light and the
              distortions
                          of light as
the flame-night
              dawns
                          Zenith-time and the anger
unto death and the
              fire-focused
                          image
of a man
              invisible man
                          and black boy and native
son and the
              man who
                          lives underground whose
name nobody
              knows
                          harrowing havocking
running through
              holocaust
                          seeking the
soul-country of his
              meaning

IX

As the gook woman howls
for her boy in the smouldering,
as the expendable Clean-Cut Boys
From Decent American Homes
are slashing off enemy ears for keepsakes;

as the victories are tallied up
with flag-draped coffins, plastic bodybags,
what can I say
but this, this:

We must not be frightened nor cajoled
into accepting evil as deliverance from evil.
We must go on struggling to be human,
though monsters of abstraction
police and threaten us.

Reclaim now, now renew the vision of
a human world where godliness
is possible and man
is neither gook nigger honkey wop nor kike

but man

permitted to be man.

X
and all the atoms cry aloud

I bear Him witness now
Who by the light of suns beyond the suns beyond
    the sun with shrill pen

    revealed renewal of
the covenant of timelessness with time, proclaimed
    advent of splendor joy

    alone can comprehend
and the imperious evils of an age could not
    withstand and stars

    and stones and seas
acclaimed—His life its crystal image and
    magnetic field.

    I bear Him witness now—
mystery Whose major clues are the heart of man,
    the mystery of God:

    Bahá'u'lláh:
Logos, poet, cosmic hero, surgeon, architect
    of our hope of peace,

    Wronged, Exiled One,
chosen to endure what agonies of knowledge, what
    auroral dark

        bestowals of truth
vision power anguish for our future's sake.
        "I was but a man

        "like others, asleep upon
My couch, when, lo, the breezes of the All-Glorious
were wafted over Me. . . ."

        Called, as in dead of night
a dreamer is roused to help the helpless flee
        a burning house.

        I bear Him witness now:
toward Him our history in its disastrous quest
        for meaning is impelled.

Monet's "Waterlilies"

(for Bill and Sonja)

Today as the news from Selma and Saigon
poisons the air like fallout,
    I come again to see
the serene great picture that I love.

Here space and time exist in light
the eye like the eye of faith believes.
    The seen, the known
dissolve in iridescence, become
illusive flesh of light
    that was not, was, forever is.

O light beheld as through refracting tears.
Here is the aura of that world
    each of us has lost.
Here is the shadow of its joy.

The Lions

With what panache, he said,
I bow to the applause,
     I open danger's door
while brasses hold their Ahs
     and set the mood
for courage leonine.
And in the kingdom-cage
as I make my lions leap,
     through nimbus-fire leap,
oh, as I see them leap—
     unsparing beauty that
creates and serves my will,
     the savage real that clues
my vision of the real—
     my soul exults and Holy cries
and Holy Holy cries, he said.

October

I
October—
its plangency, its glow

as of words in
the poet's mind,

as of God in
the saint's.

II

I wept for your mother
in her pain, wept in
my joy when you were
born,
      Maia,
that October morning.
We named you
for a star a star-like
poem sang.
        I write this
for your birthday
and say I love you
and say October
like the phoenix sings you.

III
This chiming
and tolling
    of lion
and phoenix
and chimera
    colors.
This huntsman's
horn, sounding
    mort for
quarry fleeing
through mirrors
    of burning
into deathless
    dying.

IV

Rockweight
of surprising snow

crushed
the October trees,

broke
branches that

crashing set
the snow on fire.

The Return
(after Pasternak)

Rooms are grotesque with furniture of snow,
ice blisters the hair of portraits;
spiderwebs of snow and ice
are skeleton stars in wolf-wind gloom.

Faces, voices, books we loved.
There were violets in Chinese bowls.
And, ah, the dancers—

they would hunt us down tonight,
they would caper on our graves.
We lived here—when?—under a spell.
We have awakened. We are here.

"Lear Is Gay"
(in memory of Betsy)

That gaiety oh
that gaiety I love
has white hair
or thinning or none,

has limbs askew
often as not,
has dimming sight.
Can manage, can

in fevers, rags,
decrepitude.
And oh can laugh
sometimes

at time as at
a scarecrow whose
hobo shoulders are
a-twitch with crows.

A Plague of Starlings
(Fisk Campus)

Evenings I hear
the workmen fire
into the stiff
magnolia leaves,
routing the starlings
gathered noisy and
befouling there.

Their scissoring
terror like glass
coins spilling breaking
the birds explode
into mica sky
raggedly fall
to ground rigid
in clench of cold.

The spared return,
when the guns are through,
to the spoiled trees
like choiceless poor
to a dangerous
dwelling place,
chitter and quarrel
in the piercing dark
above the killed.

Mornings, I pick
my way past death's
black droppings:
on campus lawns
and streets
the troublesome
starlings
frost-salted lie,
troublesome still.

And if not careful
I shall tread
upon carcasses
carcasses when I
go mornings now
to lecture on
what Socrates,
the hemlock hour nigh,
told sorrowing
Phaedo and the rest
about the migratory
habits of the soul.

The Night-Blooming Cereus (1972)

ि≥

For John and Margaret Thompson

Richard Hunt's "Arachne"

Human face becoming locked insect face
  mouth of agony shaping a cry it cannot utter
    eyes bulging brimming with the horrors
     of her becoming

    Dazed crazed
   by godly vivisection husking her
  gutting her
cutting hubris its fat and bones away

In goggling terror fleeing powerless to flee
  Arachne not yet arachnid and no longer woman
   in the moment's centrifuge of dying
    becoming

The Night-Blooming Cereus

And so for nights
we waited, hoping to see
the heavy bud
        break into flower.

On its neck-like tube
hooking down from the edge
of the leaf-branch
        nearly to the floor,

the bud packed
tight with its miracle swayed
stiffly on breaths
        of air, moved

as though impelled
by stirrings within itself.
It repelled as much
        as it fascinated me

sometimes—snake,
eyeless bird head,
beak that would gape
        with grotesque life-squawk.

But you, my dear,
conceded less to the bizarre
than to the imminence
        of bloom. Yet we agreed

we ought
to celebrate the blossom,
paint ourselves, dance
        in honor of
114

archaic mysteries
when it appeared. Meanwhile
we waited, aware
    of rigorous design.

Backster's
polygraph, I thought,
would have shown
    (as clearly as it had

a philodendron's
fear) tribal sentience
in the cactus, focused
    energy of will.

That belling of
tropic perfume—that
signalling
    not meant for us;

the darkness
cloyed with summoning
fragrance. We dropped
    trivial tasks

and marvelling
beheld at last the achieved
flower. Its moonlight
    petals were

still unfold-
ing, the spike fringe of the outer
perianth recessing
    as we watched.

Lunar presence,
foredoomed, already dying,
it charged the room
  with plangency

  older than human
cries, ancient as prayers
invoking Osiris, Krishna,
  Tezcátlipóca.

  We spoke
in whispers when
we spoke
  at all . . .

The Performers

Easily, almost matter-of-factly they step,
two minor Wallendas, with pail and squeegee along
the wintry ledge, hook their harness to the wall
and leaning back into a seven-story angle of space
begin washing the office windows. I
am up there too until straps break
and iron paper apple of iron I fall
through plateglass wind onto stalagmites below.

But am safely at my desk again by the time
the hairline walkers, high-edge
balancers end their center-ring routine
and crawl inside. A rough day, I remark,
for such a risky business. Many thanks.
Thank *you*, sir, one of the men replies.

The Peacock Room
(in memory of Betsy Graves Reyneau)

Ars Longa   Which is crueller
Vita Brevis   life or art?
     Thoughts in the Peacock Room,
where briefly I shelter. As in the glow
(remembered or imagined?)
     of the lamp shaped like a rose
my mother would light
for me some nights to keep
     Raw-Head-And-Bloody-Bones away.

Exotic, fin de siècle, unreal
and beautiful the Peacock Room.
     Triste metaphor.
Hiroshima   Watts   My Lai.
Thus history scorns
     the vision chambered in gold
and Spanish leather, lyric space;
rebukes, yet cannot give the lie
     to what is havened here.

Environment as ornament.
Whistler with arrogant art designed
     it, mocking a connoisseur
with satiric arabesque of gold
peacocks on a wall peacock blue
     in fury trampling coins of gold.
Such vengeful harmonies drove
a rival mad. As in a dream
     I see the crazed young man.

He shudders in a corner, shields
his face in terror of
        the perfect malice of those claws.
She too is here—ghost
of the happy child she was that day.
        When I turned twelve,
they gave me for a birthday gift
a party in the Peacock Room.
        With shadow cries

the peacocks flutter down,
their spread tails concealing her,
        then folding, drooping to reveal
her eyeless, old—Med School
cadaver, flesh-object
        pickled in formaldehyde,
who was artist, compassionate,
clear-eyed. Who was belovéd friend.
        No more. No more.

The birds resume their splendored pose.
And Whistler's portrait of
        a tycoon's daughter gleams
like imagined flowers. What is art?
What is life?
        What the Peacock Room?
Rose-leaves and ashes drift
its portals, gently spinning toward
        a bronze Bodhisattva's ancient smile.

Smelt Fishing

In the cold spring night
the smelt are spawning. Sportsmen
fevered crowd the lake.

II

Thin snow scatters on
the wind, melting as it falls.
Cries for help for light.

III

Who is he night-
waters entangle, reclaim?
Blank fish-eyes.

"Dance the Orange"
(Rilke)

And dance this
boneharp tree

and dance this
boneflower tree

tree in the
snowlight

miming a dancer
dancing a tree

Traveling through Fog

Looking back, we cannot see,
except for its blurring lights
like underwater stars and moons,
our starting-place.
Behind us, beyond us now
is phantom territory, a world
abstract as memories of earth
the traveling dead take home.
Between obscuring cloud
and cloud, the cloudy dark
ensphering us seems all we can
be certain of. Is Plato's cave.

Angle of Ascent (1975)

කම

In memory of
Roanne and Richard

Beginnings

I
Plowdens, Finns,
Sheffeys, Haydens,
Westerfields.

Pennsylvania gothic,
Kentucky homespun,
Virginia baroque.

II

A shotgun on his shoulder,
his woman big with child and
shrieking curses after him,

Joe Finn came down from
Allegheny wilderness
to join Abe Lincoln's men.

Goddamning it survives the
slaughter at the Crater.
Disappears into his name.

III
Greatgrandma Easter, on my father's side,
was a Virginia freedman's Indian bride.
She was more than six feet tall. At ninety could
still chop and tote firewood.

IV

Great-aunt Sally, great-aunt Melisse—
how they danced and sang in that hoo-rah's house.
Sold their parlor chairs to go
to Billy Kersands' minstrel show;
crooned and shuffled when they came back home,
Brother Tambo, Brother Bones.

Melissabelle and Sarah Jane
oh they took all the prizes one Hallowe'en.
And we'll let the calico curtain fall
on Pocahontas and the Corncob Queen
dancing the figures the callers call—
Sashay, ladies, promenade, all.

V

(The Crystal Cave Elegy)

Floyd Collins oh
I guess he's a goner,
Pa Hayden sighed,
the Extra trembling
in his hands.
Poor game loner
trapped in the rock
of Crystal Cave, as
once in Kentucky coal-
mine dark (I taste the
darkness yet)
my greenhorn dream of
life. Alive down there
in his grave. Open
for him, blue door.

Free Fantasia: Tiger Flowers
(for Michael)

The sporting people
along St. Antoine—
that scufflers'
paradise of ironies—
    bet salty money
on his righteous
    hook and jab.

I was a boy then, running
(unbeknownst to Pa)
errands for Miss Jackie
and Stack-o'-Diamonds' Eula Mae.
. . . Their perfumes,
rouged Egyptian faces.
    Their pianolas jazzing.

O Creole babies,
Dixie odalisques,
speeding through cutglass
dark to see the macho angel
    trick you'd never
turn, his bluesteel prowess
    in the ring.

Hardshell believers
amen'd the wreck
as God A'mighty's
will. I'd thought
    such gaiety could not
die. Nor could our
    elegant avenger.

The Virgin Forest
by Rousseau—
its psychedelic flowers
towering, its deathless
        dark dream figure
death the leopard
        claws—I choose it
now as elegy
        for Tiger Flowers.

For a Young Artist

Sprawled in the pigsty,
      snouts nudging snuffling him—
a naked old man
      with bloodstained wings.

      Fallen from the August sky?
Dead? Alive?
      But he twists away

from the cattle-prod, wings
      jerking, lifts his grizzled head,
regarding all
      with searching eyes.

Neither smiles nor threats,
dumbshow nor lingua franca
were of any use to those
trying for clues to him.

They could not make him hide
his nakedness
in their faded hand-me-downs.

Humane, if hostile and afraid,
they spread him a pallet
in the chicken-house.
The rooster pecked his wings.

Leftovers were set out for him;
he ate sunflowers
instead and the lice crawling his feathers.

Carloads of the curious paid
his clever hosts to see the
actual angel? carny freak?
in the barbedwire pen.

They crossed themselves and prayed
his blessing;
catcalled and chunked at him.

In the dark his heavy wings
open and shut, stiffly spread
like a wooden butterfly's.

He leaps, board wings clum-
sily flapping, big sex
flopping, falls.

The hawk-haunted fowl
flutter and squawk;
panic squeals in the sty.

He strains, an awk-
ward patsy, sweating strains
leaping falling. Then—

silken rustling in the air,
the angle of ascent
achieved.

Stars

I
Stood there then among
spears and kindled shields,
praising Orion.

II
Betelgeuse Aldebaran

Abstract as future yesterdays
        the starlight
crosses eons of meta-space
        to us.

    Algol Arcturus Almaak

How shall the mind keep warm
        save at spectral
fires—how thrive but by the light
        of paradox?

    Altair Vega Polaris Maia

III
(Sojourner Truth)

Comes walking barefoot
out of slavery

ancestress
childless mother

following the stars
her mind a star

IV
Pulsars, blue receding
quasars—their vibrant
radio waves.
Cosmic Ouija,
what is the
mathematics of your message?

V
(The Nine-Pointed Star)

Stable stars, variable stars—
hydrogen-into-helium
fusions, radiations, spectral fires.

And the Nine-Pointed Star,
sun star in the constellation
of the nuclear Will;

fixed star whose radiance
filtering down to us lights mind and
spirit, signals future light.

Two Egyptian Portrait Masks

I. *Nefert-iti*

A memory
carved on stelae of
the city Akhenaten built for God—

> Fair of face   Joyous with the Double Plume
> Mistress of Happiness   Endowed
> with Favor   at hearing whose Voice
>
> one rejoices   Lady of Grace
> Great of Love   whose disposition cheers
> the Lord of Two Lands—

whose burntout
loveliness alive in stone
is like the fire of precious stones

dynastic
death (gold mask and vulture wings)
charmed her with so she would never die.

II. *Akhenaten*

Upon the
mountain Aten spoke
and set the spirit moving

in the
Pharaoh's heart: O Lord of every land
shining forth for all:

Aten
multi-single like the sun
reflecting Him by Him

reflected.
Anubis howled. The royal prophet reeled
under the dazzling weight

of vision,
exalted—maddened?—the spirit moving
in his heart: Aten Jahveh Allah God.

Butterfly Piece
(for Robert Stilwell)

Brazilian butterflies, static and perfect as
      enamelwork by Fabergé. Jewel corpses fixed
in glass. Black opal flowerskin banded
      neargold yellow; sea-agate striped berylgreen;

      Colors so intense I imagine them heavy enough
           to have broken the live wings—as human
      colors in our inhuman world burden, break.

           Occult prismatic blue of the Morpho,
                 the great prized Morpho that living seems
           conjured forth by magic hands. Wild beauty
                killed, sold to prettify.

The Moose Wallow

Friends warned of moose that
often came to the wallow
near the path I took.

I feared, hoped to see
the tall ungainly creatures
in their battle crowns.

I felt their presence
in the dark (hidden watchers)
on either side.

Crispus Attucks

Name in a footnote. Faceless name.
Moot hero shrouded in Betsy Ross
and Garvey flags—propped up
by bayonets, forever falling.

American Journal (1978), (1982)

❧

For Robert Burns Stepto,
for Stephen and Danny Dunning

in love and service evermore

For Michael S. Harper,
for William Meredith—
        sustainers

A Letter from Phillis Wheatley
London, 1773

Dear Obour
        Our crossing was without
event. I could not help, at times,
reflecting on that first—my Destined—
voyage long ago (I yet
have some remembrance of its Horrors)
and marvelling at God's Ways.
        Last evening, her Ladyship presented me
to her illustrious Friends.
I scarce could tell them anything
of Africa, though much of Boston
and my hope of Heaven. I read
my latest Elegies to them.
"O Sable Muse!" the Countess cried,
embracing me, when I had done.
I held back tears, as is my wont,
and there were tears in Dear
Nathaniel's eyes.
        At supper—I dined apart
like captive Royalty—
the Countess and her Guests promised
signatures affirming me
True Poetess, albeit once a slave.
Indeed, they were most kind, and spoke,
moreover, of presenting me
at Court (I thought of Pocahontas)—
an Honor, to be sure, but one,
I should, no doubt, as Patriot decline.
        My health is much improved;
I feel I may, if God so Wills,
entirely recover here.
Idyllic England! Alas, there is
no Eden without its Serpent. Under

the chiming Complaisance I hear him Hiss;
I see his flickering tongue
when foppish would-be Wits
murmur of the Yankee Pedlar
and his Cannibal Mockingbird.
  Sister, forgive th'intrusion of
my Sombreness—Nocturnal Mood
I would not share with any save
your trusted Self. Let me disperse,
in closing, such unseemly Gloom
by mention of an Incident
you may, as I, consider Droll:
Today, a little Chimney Sweep,
his face and hands with soot quite Black,
staring hard at me, politely asked:
"Does you, M'lady, sweep chimneys too?"
I was amused, but dear Nathaniel
(ever Solicitous) was not.
  I pray the Blessings of our Lord
and Saviour Jesus Christ be yours
Abundantly. In His Name,

                    Phillis

John Brown

I
Loved feared hated:
aureoled
in violence.

Foredoomed to fail
in all but the prophetic
task?
Axe in Jehovah's
loving wrathful hand?

The face is not cruel,
the eyes are not mad but
unsparing;
the life
has the symmetry
of a cross:
John Brown
Ossowatomie   De Old Man.

II

Doing The Lord's work with sabre
sharpened on the grindstone
of The Word:
                    Bleeding Kansas:

the cries of my people the cries
of their oppressors harrowed
hacked—poison meat for Satan's
maw.
        I slew no man but blessed
the Chosen, who in the name
of justice killed at my command.

Bleeding Kansas:
                    a son martyred
there: I am tested I am trued
made worthy of my servitude.

Oh the crimes of this guilty
guilty land:
                    let Kansas bleed.

III
Fury of truth: fury
of righteousness
become
            angelic evil
demonic good?
            My hands
are bloody who never wished
to kill wished only to obey
The Higher Law.
            Fury
of truth, its enigmas,
its blinding
            illuminations.

IV

fire harvest: John Brown
and his Chosen
            at Harper's Ferry:
fury of The Word made pikes guns
swords:
            Arm the slaves
seize their masters kill
only if you must:

bloodburst: bloodflow:

Who sent you here, John Brown?
None in human form.

Fire harvest: harvest fire:

spent forlorn colossal
in that bloody light
death-agonies around him
Gabriel and Nat
awaiting him:
            I have failed:
Come, Death, breathe life
into my Cause, O Death.

v

And now
             these mordant images—

these vibrant stainedglass
colors, elemental shapes
in ardent interplay
with what we know of him
know yet fail to understand—
even we
             for whom he died:

(Shall we not say he died
for us?)

Hanged body turning clockwise
in the air
             the hour
speeding to that hour
his dead-of-night
sorrows visions prophesied:

And now
             these haunting stark
torchlight images:

Theory of Evil

Big Harpe, Little Harpe—
you met them on
the Natchez Trace
you'd stare into mystic
evil's face.
Oh wouldn't live
to say you had,
or if you lived
could only gasp
with hurting breath—
Them Harpes—
before delirium and death.

Po' wayfaring
stranger, none
to ease his moans,
Big Harpe slashed
him open, filled
his belly with stones
then left him for
the river to eat.

(We think of that
as we follow the Trace
from Nashville down
to Jackson—muse
on the cussedness
of the human race.)

When Big Harpe's head
had been cut off,
they took and nailed it
to a sycamore tree.
(Buzzards gathered
but would not feed.)
It crooned in its festering,
sighed in its withering—
Almighty God
He fashioned me
for to be a scourge,
the scourge of all humanity.

Paul Laurence Dunbar
(for Herbert Martin)

We lay red roses on his grave,
speak sorrowfully of him
as if he were but newly dead

And so it seems to us
this raw spring day, though years
before we two were born he was
a young poet dead.

Poet of our youth—
his "cri du coeur" our own,
his verses "in a broken tongue"

beguiling as an elder
brother's antic lore.
Their sad blackface lilt and croon
survive him like

The happy look (subliminal
of victim, dying man)
a summer's tintypes hold.

The roses flutter in the wind;
we weight their stems
with stones, then drive away.

Homage to Paul Robeson

Call him deluded, say that he
was dupe and by half-truths betrayed.
I speak him fair in death,
remembering the power of his
compassionate art. All else fades.

The Rag Man
(for Herbert)

In scarecrow patches and tatters, face
to the wind, the Rag Man walks
the winter streets, ignoring the cold
that for weeks has been so rigorous
we begin to think it a punishment
for our sins—a dire warning at the very least.

He strides on in his rags and word-
less disdain as though wrapped in fur,
noted stranger who long since
(the story goes) rejected all
that we risk chills and fever and cold
hearts to keep. Who is he really, the Rag Man?

Where is he going or coming from?
He would not answer if we asked,
refusing our presence as he would
our brief concern. We'd like to buy
him a Goodwill overcoat, a bowl of soup;
and, yes, we'd like to get shut of the sight of him.

The Prisoners

Steel doors—guillotine gates—
of the doorless house closed massively.
We were locked in with loss.

Guards frisked us, marked our wrists,
then let us into the drab Rec Hall—
splotched green walls, high windows barred—

where the dispossessed awaited us.
Hands intimate with knife and pistol,
hands that had cruelly grasped and throttled

clasped ours in welcome. I sensed the plea
of men denied: Believe us human
like yourselves, who but for Grace. . . .

We shared reprieving Hidden Words
revealed by the Godlike imprisoned
One, whose crime was truth.

And I read poems I hoped were true.
It's like you been there, brother, been there,
the scarred young lifer said.

The Tattooed Man

I gaze at you,
longing longing,
as from a gilt
and scarlet cage;
silent, speak
your name, cry—
Love me.
To touch you, once
to hold you close—
My jungle arms,
their prized chimeras,
appall. You fear
the birds-of-paradise
perched on my thighs.

Oh to break through,
to free myself—
lifer in The Hole—
from servitude
I willed. Or was
it evil circumstance
that drove me to seek
in strangeness strange
abiding-place?
Born alien,
homeless everywhere,
did I, then, choose
bizarrity,
having no other choice?

Hundreds have paid
to gawk at me—
grotesque outsider whose
unnaturalness
assures them they
are natural, they indeed
belong.
But you but you,
for whom I would
endure caustic acids,
keenest knives—
you look at me with pain,
avert your face,
love's own,
ineffable and pure
and not for gargoyle
kisses such as mine.

Da Vinci's Last Supper—
a masterpiece
in jewel colors
on my breast
(I clenched my teeth in pain;
all art is pain
suffered and outlived);
gryphons, naked Adam
embracing naked Eve,
a gaiety of imps
in cinnabar;
the Black Widow
peering from the web
she spun, belly to groin—
These that were my pride

repel the union of
your flesh with mine.

I yearn I yearn.
And if I dared
the agonies
of metamorphosis,
would I not find
you altered then?
I do not want
you other than you are.
And I—I cannot
(will not?) change.
It is too late
for any change
but death.
I am I.

Elegies for Paradise Valley

1

My shared bedroom's window
opened on alley stench.
A junkie died in maggots there.
I saw his body shoved into a van.
I saw the hatred for our kind
glistening like tears
in the policemen's eyes.

No place for Pestalozzi's
fiorelli. No time of starched
and ironed innocence. Godfearing
elders, even Godless grifters, tried
as best they could to shelter
us. Rats fighting in their walls.

III
Waxwork Uncle Henry
(murdered Uncle Crip)
lay among floral pieces
in the front room where
the Christmas tree had stood.

Mister Hong of the
Chinese Lantern (there
Auntie as waitress queened it
nights) brought freesias, wept
beside the coffin.

Beautiful, our neighbors
murmured; he would be proud.
Is it mahogany?
Mahogany—I'd heard
the victrola voice of

dead Bert Williams
talk-sing that word as macabre
music played, chilling
me. Uncle Crip
had laughed and laughed.

IV

Whom now do you guide, Madam Artelia?
Who nowadays can summon you to speak
from the spirit place your ghostly home
of the oh-riental wonders there—
of the fate, luck, surprises, gifts

awaiting us out here? Oh, Madam,
part Seminole and confidante
("Born with a veil over my face")
of all our dead, how clearly you
materialize before the eye

of memory—your AfroIndian features,
Gypsy dress, your silver crucifix
and manycolored beads. I see
again your waitingroom, with its wax
bouquets, its plaster Jesus of the Sacred Heart.

I watch blue smoke of incense curl
from a Buddha's lap as I wait with Ma
and Auntie among your nervous clients.
You greet us, smiling, lay your hand
in blessing on my head, then lead

the others into a candlelit room
I may not enter. She went into a trance,
Auntie said afterward, and spirits
talked, changing her voice to suit
their own. And Crip came.

Happy yes I am happy here,
he told us; dying's not death. Do not grieve.
Remembering, Auntie began to cry
and poured herself a glass of gin.
Didn't sound a bit like Crip, Ma snapped.

166

V

And Belle the classy dresser, where is she,
who changed her frocks three times a day?
Where's Nora, with her laugh, her comic flair,
stagestruck Nora waiting for her chance?
Where's fast Iola, who so loved to dance
she left her sickbed one last time to whirl
in silver at The Palace till she fell?
Where's mad Miss Alice, who ate from garbage cans?
Where's snuffdipping Lucy, who played us 'chunes'
on her guitar? Where's Hattie? Where's Melissabelle?
Let vanished rooms, let dead streets tell.

Where's Jim, Watusi prince and Good Old Boy,
who with a joke went off to fight in France?
Where's Tump the defeated artist, for meals or booze
daubing with quarrelsome reds, disconsolate blues?
Where's Les the huntsman? Tough Kid Chocolate, where
is he? Where's dapper Jess? Where's Stomp the shell-
shocked, clowning for us in parodies of war?
Where's taunted Christopher, sad queen of night?
And Ray, who cursing crossed the color line?
Where's gentle Brother Davis? Where's dopefiend Mel?
Let vanished rooms, let dead streets tell.

VI

Of death. Of loving too:
Oh sweet sweet jellyroll:
so the sinful hymned it while
the churchfolk loured.

I scrounged for crumbs:
I yearned to touch the choirlady's hair,
I wanted Uncle Crip

to kiss me, but he danced
with me instead;
we Balled-the-Jack
to Jellyroll

Morton's brimstone
piano on the phonograph,
laughing, shaking the gasolier
a later stillness dimmed.

VII

Our parents warned us: Gypsies
kidnap you. And we must never play
with Gypsy children: Gypsies
all got lice in their hair.

Their queen was dark as Cleopatra
in the Negro History Book. Their king's
sinister arrogance flashed fire
like the diamonds on his dirty hands.

Quite suddenly he was dead,
his tribe clamoring in grief.
They take on bad as Colored Folks,
Uncle Crip allowed. Die like us too.

Zingaros: Tzigeune: Gitanos: Gypsies:
pornographers of gaudy otherness:
aliens among the alien: thieves,
carriers of sickness: like us like us.

VIII

Of death, of loving,
of sin and hellfire too.
Unsaved, old Christians
gossiped; pitched

from the gamblingtable—
Lord have mercy on
his wicked soul—
face foremost into hell.

We'd dance there, Uncle
Crip and I,
for though I spoke
my pieces well in Sunday School,

I knew myself (precocious
in the ways of guilt
and secret pain)
the devil's own rag babydoll.

Names

Once they were sticks and stones
I feared would break my bones:
Four Eyes. And worse.
Old Four Eyes fled
to safety in the danger zones
Tom Swift and Kubla Khan traversed.

When my fourth decade came,
I learned my name was not my name.
I felt deserted, mocked.
Why had the old ones lied?
No matter. They were dead.

And the name on the books was dead,
like the life my mother fled,
like the life I might have known.
You don't exist—at least
not legally, the lawyer said.
As ghost, double, alter ego then?

Double Feature

At Dunbar, Castle or Arcade
we rode with the exotic sheik
through deserts of erotic flowers;
held in the siren's madonna arms
were safe from the bill-collector's power.

Forgave the rats and roaches we
could not defeat, beguiled by jazzbo
strutting of a mouse. And when
the Swell Guy, roused to noblest wrath,
shot down all those weakéd men,

Oh how we cheered to see the good we were
destroy the bad we'd never be.
What mattered then the false, the true
at Dunbar, Castle or Arcade,
where we were other for an hour or two?

The Dogwood Trees
(for Robert Slagle)

Seeing dogwood trees in bloom,
I am reminded, Robin,
of our journey through the mountains
in an evil time.

Among rocks and rock-filled streams
white bracts of dogwood
clustered. Beyond, nearby, shrill slums
were burning,

the crooked crosses flared. We drove
with bitter knowledge
of the odds against comradeship we dared
and were at one.

Letter

It was as though you struggled against
fierce current jagged with debris
to save me then. I am desperate still.
Old age—the elegy time—that brings
a sense of shores receding? But no.
What rends my spirit like beast-
angel, angel-beast has for
a lifetime nurtured and tormented me.

—This tells you nothing, tells you all,
leaves unresolved a thing absurd,
in truth grotesque. You have risked pain
because of it, are yet compassionate.
I will no longer ask for more
than you have freely given or can give.

Ice Storm

Unable to sleep, or pray, I stand
by the window looking out
at moonstruck trees a December storm
has bowed with ice.

Maple and mountain ash bend
under its glassy weight,
their cracked branches falling upon
the frozen snow.

The trees themselves, as in winters past,
will survive their burdening,
broken thrive. And am I less to You,
my God, than they?

"As My Blood Was Drawn"

As my blood was drawn,
as my bones were scanned,
the People of Bahá
were savaged were slain;

skeletons were gleaning
famine fields,
horrors multiplying
like cancer cells.

World I have loved,
so lovingly hated,
is it your evil
that has invaded
my body's world?

As surgeons put
me to the knife,
innocents
were sacrificed.

I woke from a death
as exiles drowned.
I called on the veiled
irradiant One.

As spreading oilslicks
burned the seas,
the doctors confirmed
metastasis.

World I have loved
and loving hated,
is it your sickness
luxuriating
in my body's world?

In dreams of death
I call upon
the irradiant veiled
terrible One.

Killing the Calves

Threatened by abundance, the ranchers
with tightfaced calculation
throw the bawling calves into a ditch and
shoot them in order to fatten the belly of cost.

The terror of the squandered calves mingles
with the terrible agony of the starving
whom their dying will not save.
Of course, the killing is "quick and clean";
and though there is no comparison reminds us

nonetheless—men women children
forced like superfluous animals
into a pit and less than cattle
in warcrazed eyes like crazed cattle slaughtered.

The Year of the Child
(for my Grandson)

And you have come,
Michael Ahman, to share
your life with us.
We have given you
an archangel's name—
and a great poet's;
we honor too
Abyssinian Ahman,
hero of peace.

May these names
be talismans;
may they invoke divine
magic to protect
you, as we cannot,
in a world that is
no place for a child—

that had no shelter
for the children in Guyana
slain by hands
they trusted; no succor
for the Biafran
child with swollen belly
and empty begging-bowl;
no refuge for the child
of the Warsaw ghetto.

What we yearned
but were powerless to do
        for them, oh we
will dare, Michael, for you,
        knowing our need
of unearned increments
        of grace.

        I look into your
brilliant eyes, whose gaze
        renews, transforms
each common thing, and hope
        that inner vision
will intensify
        their seeing. I am
content meanwhile to have
        you glance at me
sometimes, as though, if you
        could talk, you'd let
us in on a subtle joke.

        May Huck and Jim
attend you. May you walk
        with beauty before you,
beauty behind you, all
        around you, and
The Most Great Beauty keep
        you His concern.

The Point
(Stonington, Connecticut)

Land's end. And sound and river come
together, flowing to the sea.
Wild swans, the first I've ever seen,
cross the Point in translucent flight.
On lowtide rocks terns gather;
sunbathers gather on the lambent shore.

All for a moment seems inscribed
on brightness, as on sunlit
bronze and stone, here at land's end,
praise for dead patriots of Stonington;
we are for an instant held in shining
like memories in the mind of God.

Zinnias
(for Mildred Harter)

Gala, holding on
  to their harvest and wine
    colors
with what seems
  bravura
    persistence:

    We would
  scarcely present
bouquets of them
  to Nureyev
    or Leontyne Price:

Yet isn't
  their hardy elan one way
    of exclaiming
More More More
  as a gala
    performance ends?

The Islands
(for Steve and Nancy, Allen and Magda)

Always this waking dream of palmtrees,
magic flowers—of sensual joys
like treasures brought up from the sea.

Always this longing, this nostalgia
for tropic islands we
have never known and yet recall.

We look for ease upon these islands named
to honor holiness; in their chromatic
torpor catch our breath.

Scorn greets us with promises of rum,
hostility welcomes us to bargain sales.
We make friends with Flamboyant trees.

Jamaican Cynthie, called alien by dese lazy
islanders—wo'k hahd, treated bad,
oh, mahn, I tellin you. She's full

of raucous anger. Nevertheless brings gifts of
scarlet hibiscus when she comes to clean,
white fragrant spider-lilies too sometimes.

The roofless walls, the tidy ruins
of a sugar mill. More than cane
was crushed. But I am tired today

of history, its patina'd cliches
of endless evil. Flame trees.
The intricate sheen of waters flowing into sun.

I wake and see
the morning like a god
in peacock-flower mantle dancing

on opalescent waves—
and can believe my furies have
abandoned for a time their long pursuit.

Bone-Flower Elegy

In the dream I enter the house
    wander vast rooms that are
        catacombs midnight subway
          cavernous ruined movie-palace
       where presences in vulture masks
         play scenes of erotic violence
           on a scaffold stage   I want
     to stay and watch but know somehow
I must not linger and come to the funeral
        chamber   in its icy nonlight see
       a naked corpse
          turning with sensual movements
           on its coffin-bed
     I have wept for you many times
     I whisper but shrink from the arms
       that would embrace me
        and treading water reach
   arched portals opening on a desert
groves of enormous nameless flowers
       twist up from firegold sand
     skull flowers flowers of sawtooth bone
      their leaves and petals interlock
         caging me for you beastangel
        raging toward me
       angelbeast shining come
           to rend me and redeem

from THE SNOW LAMP

it is beginning oh
it begins now
breathes into me
becomes my breath

out of the dark
like seal to harpoon
at breathinghole
out of the dark

where I have wait-
ed in stillness that
prays for truth-
ful dancing words

ay-ee it breathes
into me becomes
my breath   spiritsong
of Miypaluk

he who returned to us
bringing festive speech
Miypaluk hunter of seal
and walrus and bear

and who more skilled
at building sledge
and igloo   ay-ee
the handler of dogs

the pleaser of girls
Miypaluk who came
from the strange-
ness beyond the ice

he who was Inouk
not knowing one of us

Inouk returned
to his people   ay-ee

Miypaluk Miypaluk

II

Across lunar wastes of wind and snow
Yeti's tract
   chimera's land
horizonless
   as outer space

through ice-rock sea
and valley
   (palm tree
fossils locked
in paleocrystic ice)

through darkness dire
as though God slept
in clutch of nightmare

through crystal and copper light
welcome as the smoking blood
of caribou
   desolate
as the soul's appalling night
toward Furthest North
     where all
meridians end
   toward

III
(cairn)

No sun these months. Ice-dark and cold.
Blind howling. Demonic dark that storms
the soul with visions none visionless can bear.
We are down to the last of the pemmican. Soon
must kill and eat our dogs.

The Angakok chants magic words against
evil spirits. Prepares for his descent
into the sea, there to comb the maggots from
Queen Nerrivik's hair that she send up her fish
(her chopped-off fingers) and seals lest we starve.

We struggle against the wish to die.
We use the Eskimo women to satiety, by this act
alone knowing ourselves men, not ghosts. We have
cabin fever. We quarrel with one another over
the women, grow vicious (as the childish Eskimos
do not). We are verminous. We stink like Eskimos.
We fight our wish to die.

Astronauts

Armored in oxygen,
        faceless in visors—
mirrormasks reflecting
        the mineral glare and
shadow of moonscape—
        they walk slowmotion
floatingly the lifeless
        dust of Taurus
Littrow. And Wow, they
        exclaim; oh boy, this is it.

        They sing, exulting
(though trained to be wary
        of "emotion and
philosophy"), breaking
        the calcined stillness
of once Absolute Otherwhere.

Risking edges, earthlings
        to whom only
their machines are friendly
        (and God's radar-
watching eye?), they
        labor at gathering
proof of hypothesis;
        in snowshine of sunlight
dangerous as radium
        probe detritus for clues.

What is it we wish them
to find for us, as
        we watch them on our
screens? They loom there
        heroic antiheroes,
smaller than myth and
        poignantly human.
Why are we troubled?
        What do we ask of these men?
What do we ask of ourselves?

[American Journal]

here among them   the americans   this baffling
multi people   extremes and variegations   their
noise   restlessness   their almost frightening
energy   how best describe these aliens in my
reports to The Counselors

disguise myself in order to study them unobserved
adapting their varied pigmentations   white black
red brown yellow   the imprecise and strangering
distinctions by which they live   by which they
justify their cruelties to one another

charming savages   enlightened primitives   brash
new comers lately sprung up in our galaxy   how
describe them   do they indeed know what or who
they are   do not seem to   yet no other beings
in the universe make more extravagant claims
for their importance and identity

like us they have created a veritable populace
of machines that serve and soothe and pamper
and entertain   we have seen their flags and
foot prints on the moon   also the intricate
rubbish left behind   a wastefully ingenious
people   many it appears worship the Unknowable
Essence   the same for them as for us   but are
more faithful to their machine made gods
technologists their shamans

oceans deserts mountains grain fields canyons
forests   variousness of landscapes weathers
sun light moon light as at home   much here is
beautiful   dream like vistas reminding me of

home   item   have seen the rock place known
as garden of the gods and sacred to the first
indigenes   red monoliths of home   despite
the tensions i breathe in i am attracted to
the vigorous americans   disturbing sensuous
appeal of so many   never to be admitted

something they call the american dream   sure
we still believe in it i guess   an earth man
in the tavern said   irregardless of the some
times night mare facts we always try to double
talk our way around   and its okay the dreams
okay and means whats good could be a damn sight
better   means every body in the good old u s a
should have the chance to get ahead or at least
should have three squares a day   as for myself
i do okay   not crying hunger with a loaf of
bread tucked under my arm you understand   i
fear one does not clearly follow i replied
notice you got a funny accent pal   like where
you from he asked   far from here i mumbled
he stared hard   i left

must be more careful   item   learn to use okay
their pass word   okay

crowds gathering in the streets today for some
reason obscure to me   noise and violent motion
repulsive physical contact   sentinels   pigs
i heard them called   with flailing clubs   rage
and bleeding and frenzy and screaming   machines
wailing   unbearable decibels   i fled lest

vibrations of the brutal scene do further harm
to my metabolism already over taxed

The Counselors would never permit such barbarous
confusion   they know what is best for our sereni
ty   we are an ancient race and have outgrown
illusions cherished here   item   their vaunted
liberty   no body pushes me around i have heard
them say   land of the free they sing   what do
they fear mistrust betray more than the freedom
they boast of in their ignorant pride   have seen
the squalid ghettoes in their violent cities
paradox on paradox   how have the americans
managed to survive

parades fireworks displays video spectacles
much grandiloquence much buying and selling
they are celebrating their history   earth men
in antique uniforms play at the carnage whereby
the americans achieved identity   we too recall
that struggle as enterprise of suffering and
faith uniquely theirs   blonde miss teen age
america waving from a red white and blue flower
float as the goddess of liberty   a divided
people seeking reassurance from a past few under
stand and many scorn   why should we sanction
old hypocrisies   thus dissenters   The Counse
lors would silence them

a decadent people The Counselors believe   i
do not find them decadent   a refutation not
permitted me   but for all their knowledge

power and inventiveness not yet more than raw
crude neophytes like earthlings everywhere

though i have easily passed for an american   in
bankers grey afro and dashiki long hair and jeans
hard hat yarmulke mini skirt   describe in some
detail for the amusement of The Counselors   and
though my skill in mimicry is impeccable   as
indeed The Counselors are aware   some thing
eludes me   some constant amid the variables
defies analysis and imitation   will i be judged
incompetent

america   as much a problem in metaphysics as
it is a nation earthly entity an iota in our
galaxy   an organism that changes even as i
examine it   fact and fantasy never twice the
same   so many variables

exert greater caution   twice have aroused
suspicion   returned to the ship until rumors
of humanoids from outer space   so their scoff
ing media voices termed us   had been laughed
away   my crew and i laughed too of course

confess i am curiously drawn   unmentionable   to
the americans   doubt i could exist among them for
long however   psychic demands far too severe
much violence   much that repels   i am attracted
none the less   their variousness their ingenuity
their elan vital   and that some thing   essence
quiddity   i cannot penetrate or name

Notes

Full Moon
"The Glorious One": one of the titles given to Bahá'u'lláh, prophet of the Bahá'í faith.

Dawnbreaker
"Dawnbreakers" is the title now used to designate the early Persian Bahá'ís, thousands of whom were martyred.

"Incense of the Lucky Virgin"
"High John the Conqueror": a root said to have magical properties, used by conjurers.

"From the Corpse Woodpiles, from the Ashes"
"He, who is man beatified": Bahá'u'lláh was imprisoned as a heretic in 1853.

Bahá'u'lláh in the Garden of Ridwan
He declared His mission in the Garden of Ridwan while on His way to prison and exile in 1863.

Middle Passage
Part III follows, in the main, the account of the Amistad mutiny given by Muriel Rukeyser in her biography of Willard Gibbs.

The Ballad of Nat Turner
Nat Turner led a slave revolt in Jerusalem, Virginia, in 1831.

For a Young Artist
After the story "A Very Old Man with Enormous Wings," by Gabriel García Márquez.

from THE SNOW LAMP
The subject of THE SNOW LAMP is Peary's expedition to the North Pole in 1909. Its focal character is Matthew A. Henson, co-discoverer of the Pole, who became a legend among the Greenland Eskimos (or Innuit, as they called themselves). They considered him one of their own and named him Miypaluk. The title of the poem comes from an Innuit folktale. The opening section attempts to suggest the spirit and mode of an Eskimo song-poem.

197

Index of Titles

Index of First Lines